Enid
J. Wilson's
COUNTRY
DIARY

Enid
J. Wilson's
COUNTRY
DIARY

Hodder & Stoughton
LONDON SYDNEY AUCKLAND TORONTO

Line drawings by Pavla Davey

British Library Cataloguing in Publication Data

Wilson, Enid J.
 Enid J. Wilson's country diary.
 1. Lake District (England)
 I. Title
 942.7'8085'0924   DA670.LI

 ISBN 0-340-41522-3

Foreword by Melvyn Bragg

We have a wonderfully rich tradition of country diarists and this book shows that Enid Wilson is part of it. For almost forty years she has 'poked' (her word) around her own parish, drawn here by some wild roses, there by a promise of badgers (very fond of badgers), by anything that provokes her curiosity. 'And nobody ever seems to mind at all,' she says, 'I mean they sort of realise you're a fairly harmless person and that's it.'

The result of this harmless curiosity has been a regular column to be discovered somewhere on the letters page of *The Guardian*. 'I've missed twice: once when I was in hospital: once when my husband died.' Over the years it has told the story of one woman's intimate journey through a fascinating landscape and its working people – the Lake District.

The diary began at the end of 1950, by accident. When the previous tenant of the column died – a friend of Enid's – 'my husband said, why don't you do that? I said, but I couldn't do that, I've never done anything seriously in my life. He said – try. So I wrote one or two and sent them off to A. J. Wadsworth who was *Guardian* Editor then and he said, yes, I could try, and he put me on probation. I hope I'm still out on probation but I don't now really know.'

She had married more or less straight from school, the children were grown up and so she had the time. She also, as it soon proved, had the touch, the talent, the style, the staying power and the location. She became a memorable chronicler of everyday country life.

Enid Wilson lives in Keswick, by Derwentwater, the most perfect of the lakes. The seasonal clatter of tourism passes her by: she lives in the older town – still a tight little Cumbrian community – and her paths beat well away from any crowd. It is a place which has held writers spellbound for more than two hundred years and not the least tribute to Enid Wilson is that she has succeeded in seeing it and writing about it in a fresh way.

Her background may help account for this. Her father was one of the Abraham brothers, famous as mountain photographers in the pioneering days, fine climbers themselves and mad about motors. Firms used to send him their toughest new models 'and ask him if he could smash them up if he could'. He tried. 'We used to take these cars over Honister, Hard Knott and Wrynose and so on. Once, up Hard Knott, it was an incredibly bad road then, I was eight and my sister was thirteen, and we were kicked out to take a rug and put it down for the front wheels of the car; father would get over that and then we'd whip the rug out and do it all over again!

'My father was very, very good at anything in the country. He was an ideal father to have because he would go birds-nesting on a Sunday morning when everybody else was being proper. And my mother, on the other hand, was a complete academic. She was a BSc and a good botanist as well. So between the two of them and their friends, his climbing friends and my mother's people who were artists – they were Welsh, my grandfather was a member of the Royal Academy – it was a very lucky mixture for a child. Anything I saw with my father I could check with my mother.'

Enid Wilson found her writing style by reading and re-reading. 'If you notice in Virginia Woolf's *Letters to Herself*, she keeps saying I must read so and so again. I think, quite unconsciously, if you read a lot you're bound to take colour from it although you may not know it.' Dorothy Wordsworth is a constant companion. In these days of educational controversy Enid Wilson's writing and her range of knowledge is a notable testimony to the effectiveness of self-help.

'I remember going to school,' she says with the amusement that lights up all comments about her own life. 'I thought it was the end of the world being shut in for the day. I don't know how many times I ran away – all to no good effect. I got sent back. But I had a very, very free and easy life.'

The fruits of that free and easy life now embellish *The Guardian* throughout the year. And if you go up to the Lakes, especially in the north, you may pass by an alert, amused lady, absorbed in the gathering of light on a mountain slope (and thinking over Dorothy Wordsworth's remarks on that), poking about a disused mill, looking into an empty ash tree, pinching a cutting from a rare flower or, best of all, waiting for badgers.

4 August 1987

Enid
J. Wilson's
COUNTRY
DIARY

Spring

Keswick

The badgers are getting more lively as spring comes and there are many signs of life about the setts; these are well hidden in a bracken-covered slope on the sunny side of the hill. The shaly earth at the mouth of the holes has been dragged out and, no doubt, new bedding has been taken in; badgers would not tolerate the slummy living of a fox's earth with its bones and smells. About a hundred yards away, across the fell, a new series of holes has been started. There are always clear badger roads through the bracken where they start uphill for a night's hunting, but between the old setts and the new there is a real highway. A soft stretch of mud carried one perfect print of a badger's paw, the five front pads, the big crescent-shaped hand pad behind, and even the claw marks showing, deeply indented. It is too cold to wait until dusk for the badgers to come out, but as soon as it is a little milder it will be a pleasant evening's occupation. The sound of a badger clearing its throat as it comes up to the night air and the glimmer of its white front are ample rewards for even a long wait.

Keswick

There is a new foxhound puppy at the farm. His predecessor, who hunted with the Blencathra pack in the winter and lived at the farm in the summer, had to be destroyed after a road accident, but the puppy proudly bears his name and already begins to fill his place. When he first came from the kennels, just before Christmas, he was all flopping ears and wobbling front legs, which seemed to wobble worse in the frost. The snow has left many dead sheep on the fells and the farmer brought down, for the dogs, a piece of extremely 'well hung' mutton. Farmers and huntsmen are great believers in such meat for making healthy dogs, and the pup ate his with every appearance of enjoyment. He had to be banished to the barn until the smell wore off! Now he is strong and shiny of coat with a lift to his front paws worthy of a ballet dancer.

There are still plenty of foxes about although the hunt has accounted for seventy-two this season. In a glint of afternoon sun yesterday, an old dog-fox slipped over the wall at the hilltop and crossed through the end of the new housing estate to gain the woods beyond. He was not being hunted and, no doubt, has gone that way many times before the houses were built.

Keswick   *18 May, 1951*

Spring calls up different associations for everyone, often depending on where they live. It may be blossom, lambs, or singing birds, but for me it is a colder mountain world, and the green things are the most important. The rowans are a soft green; the birches a yellow green, quite different from any other tree; the bracken fronds, those small croziers of the fellside, have touches of brown on their stems; but the most astonishing green of all is that of the green-hairstreak butterflies (*Callophrys rubi*). I had been up to a buzzard's nest in an oak wood and admired the bird's decoration of green larch round the nest edge. There are two buzzards' nests, each with eggs, within a mile of each other, and I was coming along the fell when I saw the butterflies. There must have been a dozen or so in that warm hollow, and at first it looked as if the bracken fronds themselves were moving. The faint golden tinge on the upper side of their wings showed in flight, but when they settled the green was predominant. Where the bracken stopped and the turf began the wild violets added a sharp purple – perfect relief to the green and brown. The trees and the flowers seem to have come out overnight in the 'arrowy rain', and at last it really looks like spring.

Keswick   *18 April, 1952*

The sun strikes warmly on the south-east-facing wall of the kitchen garden at the farm and uncurls the fronds of the spleenwort and wall rue. Halfway up is a deep recess, about four feet long, floored with Borrowdale stone, made to take the skeps used by beekeepers not so long ago. It is empty now and hives are used instead, but the bees' ways never change. My hives face the morning sun and the bees are soon afield. By half past eight they are on the gooseberry flowers, and as the sun rises higher their contented hum spreads to the willows at the garden's edge and the gorse on the hill. I have been spring-cleaning the hives, and when the roof and wooden walls are taken away the brood chamber is moved, the floor brushed clean, and all made neat. In the brood chamber the busy workers are tending the young bees as they come from the cells. Comparatively few are hatching as yet and the other cells are filled with pollen, which, with nectar or sugar syrup, will constitute their food. There is the lemon yellow of pussy-willow pollen, the dull yellow of gorse, the delicate green of bat willow, and, perhaps the most striking of all, the deep-red orange of pollen from the purple crocuses – a fair and glowing record of hard work and a promise of summer's plenty.

Keswick   17 April, 1953

A brisk wind comes up from the valley and over the wakening fields whose spring green is at last defeating winter's dull browns. The sun is opening the small bronze leaves on the sycamores but they are still wrinkled from their long wait in the bud. The wind and the sunlight together chase the cloud shadows across the meadow below the farm and up through the drying green where the sycamores stand and the quilts hang airing on the lines stretched from tree to tree. They shake the new leaves and set the quilts in motion, too, so that these seem to change and fold and blossom in the light. They were made in the days when life seemed more leisurely and women wore voluminous cotton dresses which often found their way eventually into the fabric of these bedcovers. One of the quilts is made of white cotton deeply banded with vivid Turkey red and firmly stitched in half moons and circles. Another is of the traditional 'box' design in which two oblongs of cotton are sewn together at one edge to make the box and a 'lid' laid across both; the sprigged 'boxes' and plain 'lids' make a mosaic of soft colour. A third quilt, of very neat patchwork, has the date when it was finished, 1872, and its first owner's initials embroidered on one edge. It was made at a now derelict farm at the head of Thirlmere and, could its owner come back today, she would see the tracks of the roads she trod as a girl, so low is the lake, and see the stones of the old farms uncovered again from the water.

Keswick *15 April, 1954*

I sat on a boulder at the foot of a crag one morning lately and watched a pair of wheatears moving restlessly from stone to stone and I admired the small green fists of the parsley fern which are uncurling so slowly in this grudging spring. The floor of the valley is a muted pattern of brown and green and, as I looked down, a large green lorry came slowly up the stony road and stopped at the end of the farm lane. It must have been expected for two men unpropped themselves from the wall and helped to lower the back of the lorry, allowing a wave of sheep to flow out.

The hoggs – last year's lambs – had come home to the valley from their wintering near the sea and there is no truer sign of the return of spring. I hurried down to meet them as they came up the lane and round the barn with a noise of bleating, a patter of hard hooves on stone, and an odd, subdued barking. I waited by the wall below the twisted plum trees which as yet can only boast a few pale flowers and saw that the farm lad himself was doing the barking! He said he did not like to use a dog when the sheep were confused from a journey. 'Turr'ble brittle laal things is hoggs,' he said, 'it's a pity it's sa often cold when they come back – it meks 'em bad t'settle.' They rested in the stone pens and towards evening I saw them again, spreading in a grey fan up the lower slopes, on their way back to the high fells.

Keswick *4 March, 1955*

The warm sun is bringing life back to the withered earth and although it is only a flush of colour in a stem, a scent on the wind, or a sound in the wood, something is there, evasive and intangible, but very real. On the lake shore the alders and the young willows dip their roots in the water, and then the land rises into a wall of tangled woodland which contains a swamp of sighing, pale-coloured reeds. At the edge of the swamp is a line of tall old willows, the tops of whose trunks have decayed to a papery whiteness which now serves to enhance the glowing olive green of their lower branches. The waxing moon hung in the north-eastern sky as pale as the willow stumps, while the sun still shone from the south-west, warming the swamp and the brown floor of the wood across which spreads wave upon wave of snowdrops whose scent, seemingly compounded of earth, water, and a green sweetness, fills the quiet air. The snowdrops have been covered by lake water, frozen, and thawed again, but they still keep their green and white beauty and in the middle of them is a group of two ash trees and a yew surrounded by arching brambles which protected, but did not conceal, a woodcock. It rested with its brown body hugged closely to the dead leaves, its eyes unwinking, until with no warning at all it rose and swerved away through the trees. It left behind it a small hollow in the leaves and, floating in the sunlight, the severed ends of spiders' threads broken by its flight and a disturbed spiral of gnats which slowly gathered again and resumed its dance.

Keswick

29 April, 1955

Spring has reached the foot of the valley where it lies in a cleft between a steep crag and a rocky hillside, but every step up seems a step back towards winter, and yet the April sky, the new golden birch leaves, the rain-washed air, and the song of the beck all have promise. Two sheep left the beckside and moved ahead of me, and when I stopped to watch the buzzards sail out from the crag I became aware of sheep voices all about me. It seemed that for reasons known only to themselves all the sheep in the valley had decided to go before me to the high land where the beck rises. They gathered in, one or two at a time, and one hogg, evidently fearing to be left behind, became so excited that it leapt breakneck down the scree baaing as it came and only slowing up for the boulders beside the path. A clean smell of rain-wet, sun-warm fleeces filled the air, and at the narrowest part of the ghyll, where there is only room for one sheep to walk at a time, the sheep voices echoed from the rocks and blotted out the buzzards' crying. Some of the creatures turned their black faces to watch the rear of the procession and then went on again, one after one, up the shelving rock ledges worn smooth through the centuries by the feet of shepherds and of sheep.

Keswick *12 April, 1956*

The ruined cottage on the moor has dignity even in decay. It seems at first sight to be a lonely place, isolated as it is a thousand feet up in a sea of nardus grass and heather, but come up under the western gable – the only standing wall – and wait; soon the sounds and the creatures of the moor will fill the solitude. A skylark sings on its upward flight; a pair of grouse move nearer through the heather until the male's red patch is plain to see and the click of beaks is audible in the heather; the beck runs quietly and all the sounds are small sounds.

It is more than thirty years since any shepherds lived here, but before that the tenancy, which belonged to a farm miles away down the valley, was unbroken from time-out-of-mind. The last baby to be born here came in early spring about sixty years ago. The neighbouring farm lads came up with lanterns from the valley – as the way was then – to hunt for the christening bowl, which had been filled with rum butter and hidden. When it was found – in the baby's cradle – it was taken down to the inn four miles away, the contents eaten, the baby's health drunk, and the customary collection filled the empty bowl. That baby got thirty-five shillings, a good sum for those times.

There are still a few shoots of rhubarb budding in the stones, a few leaves of fat-hen, and though the heather creeps nearer every year it is a place to which the swallows first return. A pair came here today and joined the skylark in the high, sweet air.

Keswick *15 March, 1957*

Lake District terriers as a breed, especially those whose forebears have been working hunt-terriers, are distinguished for their courage but not always for their caution or common sense. Three of them were out at dusk, lately, with their master when one, who had been out of sight for some time, suddenly fled – yelping and frightened – from a badger sett. It must have met the occupant. Whereupon a second terrier, only nine months old, made an eager dash for the same sett and disappeared. There was a terrible commotion underground, barking and thumping which could be heard

15

clearly on the surface, and then an ominous silence. Long after dark there was no sign of the terrier and none at dawn next morning, so after the day's work its master set out with a dachshund and together they went to the badger holes. But which hole of the sett should they dig? One was chosen but it split into four below the surface and they stopped, despondent. But not the dachshund; it suddenly erupted into barks and shot down one of the dark galleries. Its voice guided the diggers not to a badger but to a much-bitten and half-dead terrier, which had been walled in after the fight between one pile of earth it had dug through and another the badger had thrown up behind itself in its retreat. It was a happy reunion and, for the dachshund, a very proud one.

Cumberland 26 April, 1957

In the dry April weather before the bracken uncurls or the heather springs green again, the badger trods stand out boldly on the face of the fell. I waited last night on a trod above a sett where there are probably young cubs; the signs pointed to their presence in early spring and even now the badger is cautious and slow to emerge, but even if she does not come there is plenty to see, and hear, in the warm, bracken-filled hollow on the fell.

The pattern of twilight is always much the same in April, the blossom-laden cherry trees shine in the dusk, curlews call from the valley, a pheasant's voice breaks out in frequent panic, and at last the brown owls – the badgers' ushers – begin their strange noises near at hand. The time is right; slowly and in complete silence the badger moves out of its hole. Not a pebble is disturbed on the pile of dug-out earth below the hole and not a stem of bracken cracks as she goes off downhill. This silence shows, I think, that she is aware of another presence on the hill, but that she is soon back facing me, with her head stripes glimmering whiter than the cherry blossom in the dusk, also shows that she feels herself mistress of the situation. She pauses once on the earthen rampart to give a gruff little bark – perhaps a warning to the young family below – before she goes off for the night's hunting. It always seems odd that so large an animal can be so silent.

Keswick

6 May, 1958

Mist hid the tops of the hills this morning and the softness of
the air set the trout jumping in the river and made the birds
on the lake-marsh call excitedly. The light was very clear and
at first I thought it was a pheasant there in the field corner
where the last green grass grows before the bents of the
marsh take over. Then I saw it was a hare, and not only one
hare but seven, unmoving, intent on one another and
oblivious of all else, the spring madness still unassuaged. One
lay comfortably in the lee of a molehill, three others grouped
about her with two more to the right, and a darker one to the
left. This was obviously a resting time, the one on the
molehill stretched and lay back, the dark one sat up and
washed its face, cat-like, going carefully behind its ears. A
cuckoo alighted on a fence post close by and a reed bunting
scolded it from the hawthorns. Suddenly, all seven hares
were up and away, running in circles and lines and loops.
They jumped sideways and flicked themselves up in the air,
and once, when two paused together, a vicious fight broke
out, and then away they went again. Once they ran in a line
past four puzzled sheep who, as they passed a second time,
fled in panic almost as fast as the hares. Time stood still for
us, and for all the notice the animals took of our presence we
might as well have been posts or trees.

Keswick

24 April, 1959

Last night the full moon was high above the sleeping whale-
back of the fell before the lamp was lit in the farm kitchen;
and so, looking out from the shadowy interior through the
small, square window set high up in the wall, one could see
the glimmer of moonlight on the whitewashed wall of the
byre opposite, and on its green slate roof. The sycamores in
this high valley are just bursting into leaf but the cherry trees
in blossom are as white as snow, and they, too, glimmered in
the moon's effulgence. It was all very peaceful, the fire
burned low on the hearth, and the farmer's wife sat half in,
half out of the shadows. Her serenity gave no indication of
how busy – how 'thrang' she called it – the two men were
outside. There are a lot of twin lambs this year and, also, the
ewes are troubled with drop. They fall where they are and die

in a matter of hours or days unless an injection of calcium or magnesium is given according to which sort – there are two – of drop has struck the sheep. This is one of the times when things hoarded 'come in' on a farm; the farmer is carrying his injection tackle with him wherever he goes in an old gas-mask case! The foxes too are a nuisance; the crags and the screes behind the farm give them easy shelter and many lambs have gone already. I wonder if it is true, as the farmer's wife asserts, that the whitest lambs are taken first? She says that it is always the whitest lamb, or pullet, or duck which disappears from the fields, but why should it be so?

Keswick   *22 April, 1960*

The hours after sunset seem to belong to the badgers and the white owls, but last night when the radiance of the sunset was fading in crimson and grey behind the western hills the owls were out and about, calling to one another, long before the badgers had wakened on the sett beside the water. This is a strange place even by daylight: a crescent of deep water left where the river ran long ago, its edge is sheltered by ash trees and a wooded half-island stands at its centre. At dusk it takes on a life of its own, and although it is still and quiet it is far from silent; the night seems to stir with a variety of small sounds. There was the slight passage of air through the trees, the breathy voices of peewits out on the lake-marsh, and the running river only a field away. Wood anemones glimmered white in the dusk, a bat wavered in and out of the ash branches whose knobbly flowers looked oddly ornate against the sky and, as the light died, four mallards came flying down the valley with outstretched necks and whistling wings. They circled the island twice and one pair landed on the lagoon in a swish of sound, breaking the reflections and sending lines of silver running into the reeds. The waking silence settled again, but only a few minutes later a fox barked – once – near at hand, and again the ducks were up and away, quacking, to seek the safety of the open lake; and still the badgers did not come.

Keswick

How far, I wonder, does the chain of cause and effect stretch both backwards and forwards? Last year's fine spring gave the hollies a chance to set a heavy crop of berries from an unusual wealth of blossom. This past mild winter made the birds less hungry and, it seemed, there were smaller flocks of invading fieldfares and redwings, so many of the hollies are still scarlet with berries, fast getting too woody for birds to enjoy. Indeed, some of the hollies are so overberried and have so few leaves that it will be interesting to see if they survive or if they die – as many did three years ago – of their own prodigality. There will be some natural regeneration, but so many hard-berried fruits need to be eaten by a bird and to pass through its gut before they can germinate. This necessity accounts for so many lonely trees out on the fellsides, seemingly isolated from their kind. How often one sees, on some steep crag or barren slope, a holly, a rowan, or a hawthorn standing all alone – yet is it alone? I rested beside a small hawthorn this morning high on the fell in the bite of the March wind, and found under my hand a small pile of fruits nibbled by voles, and saw how the winter grass, caught in the lowest thorns, had made a form for some wandering hare. There were bird droppings on the rocks, and in the tree's roots the first delicate leaves of wood sorrel poked up – making an island of life on an otherwise barren fell.

Lake District

The level peat moss, the crag which goes steeply up some hundreds of feet above it, and the seldom-used track between the two places is, I think, typical of this district – especially at this time of the year. The birches in the moss are unfurling new green leaves; the bog myrtle has orange, pollen-bearing male cones and bright red, brush-like female flowers; the intense green of polytrichum moss is ankle-deep in places, but where the ground is drier the pale, scentless flowers of marsh violets rise from round, green leaves. This morning a comfortable red squirrel sat in one of the stunted Scots pines, nibbling seeds from cones and rattling the cores down through the branches. There were prints on the track where a badger, a fox, and even some deer had passed during the night, and the deer had left scrabbled patches of moss in the wood. As I moved up through the dark fir trees above the track towards a line of light where the scree begins in a mass of tumbled rocks, some of them half the size of a house, I startled a pair of woodcock – myself no less – in a patch of wood sorrel, and sent them swerving off through the trees. This is harder, wilder land; red-flowered blaeberry bushes, stag's-horn moss, and the first hair-like stalks of oak fern grow there. The larches and junipers are thickly hung with grey beards of lichen and the wind goes through them with a sound like the sea.

Grasmere   20 April, 1962

On 27 April, 1802, Dorothy Wordsworth wrote in her diary at Dove Cottage, Grasmere: 'A fine morning – when I came back [from a walk] I found that he [William] and John Fisher had cleaned out the well; John had sodded about the bee-stand.' The bee-stand, or rather the little house which sheltered it, is still there in the garth at Sykeside where the Fishers lived across from Dove Cottage beside the present Wordsworth Museum, and lately the Wordsworth Trust has begun a work of salvage on it. The 'house' is roofed with wrestler slates, slates notched and clicked together in the style of Cumberland and Westmorland wrestlers' hands. It has lost a little of its character perhaps now by the addition of cement, but the work is not completed yet. There is room under the roof for a bee-stand and there are two stone-lined bee boles alongside (a Scottish dictionary defines a bole, or boal, as a hole in a wall to hold small objects), and it is well worth a visit. Bee houses and bee boles are uncommon and belong mainly to the wet and mountainous third of England where stone walls and stone houses abound, and are often very old – three hundred years or more. The bees in their straw skeps were housed in the boles or on the roofed stands in summer and winter; straw covers – hackles – were added in winter to keep out the cold and replaced in summer by a cap for storing honey.

Keswick

Has the Lake District changed so very much in the last 150 years? Yes, obviously it has. Yet in some fundamental but unobtrusive ways it remains the same – or so it seems from the reports of the directors of Greenwich Hospital who made 'visitations' to their manors of Derwentwater, Castle Rigg and Thornthwaite. These lands came to them at the attainder and beheading of the last Earl of Derwentwater after the 1715 uprising. Many of the woods beside Derwentwater were planted from 1759 onwards to replace others 'getting to maturity'. The oaks there in 1805 are said to be in 'a fine thriving state', some of them still are and look good for another century or so. In 1813 the value of timber cut on some of the land was £2,115, and oak bark fetched £13 a ton. In spite of improved farming the state of much of the land is constant; one of the fields on to which my windows look was 'in need of drainage' – it still is – and others are said to be 'cold, wet land'. The names of the fields show their character: High, Low, East, and Little Springs Meadows; Sheep, Horse, Calf, and Deer Close; New Rivings and Black Steps. Where, however, can the little, humped field in the turn of the river at Nancrook have got its name of Virily? One remark brings the visitation in 1813 to life when it is said (perhaps a little smugly) that the directors exercised their right to fish by net on Derwentwater 'with more success than appears to have been met with in 1805'.

Keswick

As grey day follows grey day and the cold wind persists, it seems as if spring will never come. But the upsurge of new life is there even if it is half-hidden. The burgeoning gold of the pussy-willow catkins are obvious enough; so, too, are the green, unfolding fingers of the horse-chestnut leaves and the red elm-flowers which set free clouds of pollen. A blackbird starts early in the half-light, breathing rather than singing its first waking notes from the dark tree where its nest is – a very different sound from the agitated, nest-defending one of daylight hours. As the day grows the curlews ripple from the high fields above the valley and the fells change from grey to misty green. It is, perhaps, less easy to know that there are fox cubs on the fell where, three months ago, an urgent vixen screamed to the night sky. The hunt, a local foot-pack, disturbed her one day this week and she, no green fox, took the dogs smartly round twice inside the wood, confusing some of the pack before she paused on the edge of the planting. She sat there for a few moments, tongue lolling, seeming to weigh up the traffic on the road and the situation generally before she slipped across and over the wall to go to ground in an ancient and disused badger fortress near some cavernous rhododendrons. The huntsman, knowing her state, called off the dogs, and soon after dusk no doubt the small fox family would be reunited.

Lake District   *22 March, 1965*

An interest in wild plants and where they grow is not always an easy or a comfortable thing to have. Some of the wilder, rarer plants come too early in the year, often in bitter weather, and survive in awkward places as one might expect in these days of all-invading traffic. Some even need, at times, to be cared for to one's own discomfort, as my stone-roughened hands and bramble-torn legs testify at present. These scars were the consequence of looking after two rare hellebores (relatives of the Christmas rose) which grow on opposite sides of a rocky limestone valley on the fringe of this district. One, the stinking hellebore, which I prefer to call setterwort, is a magnificent, branching, evergreen plant with fingered leaves and down-turned, pale green flowers edged with purple. It lives in an ash copse in a treacherous fall of limestone criss-crossed with militant brambles. Early gales had battered the plants so it seemed sensible, with the flowers opening, to prop them up for the early bees to visit so that seed could be set. The other side of the valley is gentler and here the other hellebore – green hellebore, called fellon grass in the north – thrives in the shelter of a wall. Today, however, I found much of the wall fallen and had to remove piles of rock before the brilliant green, almost leafless, flowers could be found. This same wall which shelters the hellebore, shelters armies of snails which eat its seeds and spread them about, too, with the slime of their bodies – a comfortable and self-contained community.

Keswick

Skiddaw is a strange mountain, all three thousand feet of it.
The Keswick side is of shaly slate with outcrops of quartz.
Some of it is bare, some turf-covered, but there are forestry
woods too – all very dull. Its north side is very different; here
lonely sweeps of moor-grass run down to small valleys and
innumerable streams which empty into the Solway plain.
The earth is red, heavy and claggy – typical sandstone
country – and there are hidden beauties, not easy to find.
Today, in a storm of rain, I found clumps of vivid green
hellebore in flower, growing almost in the water, where two
becks meet. It was not hellebore, however, which I had gone
to hunt or even the wild daffodils near them, or the primrose
banks, but lungwort – Joseph and Mary, Adam and Eve, call
it what you will, names given by the blue and red flowers on
one plant.

I did not find the lungwort or the wild daphne which
should be there too but, almost as a consolation, a very
strange and rich tumble of woodland. Here spotted orchid
leaves jostled with columbines for living space, sweet blue
violets were just fading with dog violets, and very large
cowslips were taking their place. It was a difficult bit of
wood to get in or out of and other creatures had found it so
too. The only way was down to the beck and over a huge
fallen ash; a roe-deer had tried the same way and its body,
trapped by two ash branches, hung, decaying, over the
water. It seemed, today, as if only the deer and the birds ever
came to this place.

Cumberland

This year March certainly came in like a lamb; but one of the
wet little lambs who, at present, stay rather shiveringly close
to their mothers with not much sign of play. These are not,
to a Cumbrian, 'real' lambs for they are crosses of biggish
breeds and have Roman noses, darkish coats, and a decorous
manner – nothing like the native Herdwick, or even rough-
faced lambs, which come much later, are smaller and much
more giddy. Any lambs, however, mean spring as much as
the snowdrops or the sloshing rain. It was obvious this
evening that lambs are very much in the minds of a farmer

and his wife who retired from their farm almost a year ago. They miss their stock – 'nowt young coming-on'. They sat by their decorous house-fire. The chimney was to be swept in the morning. She said, ''lectric sweep' or no, how much easier it would have been on the farm. There, an armful of bents in the chimney and a good blaze would have done all that was needed.

They had been back to the farm – they often go – and were a bit comforted to see that the new tenant, a lad from the next farm, is keeping the spot so well and, it seems, he uses the same names for the fields: Flatts, the Bog Field, the Big Pasture, and so on. A seventeenth-century map names one of their fields as Strawberry Bank, but they did not know that name and would not accept it. Indeed, anyone who knows the valley would think strawberries out of place there – the golden lambs' tails swinging from the hazels now seem much more at home.

Keswick *20 March, 1967*

Many things were out this morning enjoying the March wind, damp though it was. A buzzard hung watchfully over the larches on the fell, breasting the gusty air, and the red squirrels feeding on the larch cones swayed precariously, their long ear-tips and busy tails blown sideways in the wind. It was quiet – or so it seemed until one sheep, then two, then a small flock began to move up the small green valley between the woods in front of a shepherd and his dog. The dog, though young, was remarkably restrained – at least at first – and man, dog and sheep moved quietly towards a gate in the wall-corner. The dog obeyed whistles for right and left and commands, 'back', 'go back, man', or 'walk up', with an air of vigour in check, and indeed it was a pattern performance until the sheep saw the wall-corner and the still-shut gate and broke like a wave of the sea.

Twice they did it, but at last all were out on the fell road and then two sheep, cusseder than the rest, suddenly charged sideways and leapt the stone wall back into their old field. They did this twice again and quite spoiled the pattern. Commands were different now, plain roars, punctuated with 'get back, you clout-head' or 'you bloody fool' and the dog even gave one of the sheep a small nip – and who could blame it? Then, almost as unpredictably, all were out and moving again up the road.

I had stood aside in the wood's edge all this time not wanting to add to the confusion and seemingly unseen, for, as the flock passed, the shepherd greeted me in a surprised sort of way. 'By,' he said, 'I nivver saw you standing there – an' I very near telled t'dog his pedigree.' But then it would not be the first 'pedigree' I had heard – nor, I hope, the last. It was quiet indeed when they all had gone.

Keswick

Mosses and mires are not so much part of this district as they are of, say, the Border or the Pennine hills, and today the big moss which lies along the foot of the Skiddaw range looked desolate and colourless in spite of a flush of umber for spring on its birch thickets. There is no white cotton-grass yet to add an ephemeral lightness to the bog, and only the pools, left where peat has been dug, give back the changing colours of the sky. The cold northerly wind has blown for weeks now, inhibiting growth. The wind slants icily round the farm at the edge of the bog, filters in through doors and windows, and creeps across the stone-flagged kitchen floor. Even the big fire of ash logs barely conquers the chill, but at mid-afternoon, with the eggs collected, the hens not yet ready to shut in for the night, and the men out milking in the byres, there is time to talk. 'It is nice,' says the farmer's wife, 'to have someone to crack with.'

The men are 'terribly quiet', and with the telly on in the evening, even the lass home from school must hush. We talked of the bog, poor land and 'sievey' (rushy) and the home of foxes, two of which lately visited the pullets, doing a lot of damage until the foot-pack came early one morning and picked up the scent by the hen houses. One fox, after a fast run, was bowled over on the fell breast: the second doubled back on its tracks to the bog and lay under the lee of a wall as the dogs, unknowingly, jumped over it – a ruse that might have succeeded had a man not seen it and given a halloo. Hunting is not an end one would wish even a fox, but with those defenceless-looking lambs out on the bog, who would care to say what else could be done?

Solway Firth

The Border between England and Scotland is still sometimes called 'The Debatable Land' – land which the Scots and English fought over, laid waste and then neglected for centuries – but the Solway Firth (that arm of water which divides the two countries in the west) is debatable too. It was for smugglers what the Border was for moss-troopers – a lawless place. So far as fishing is concerned now there are still Scottish or English waters with, roughly, the salmon-fishing rights of the former under Crown Charter and the latter vested in the River Board. But each side of the Solway has its own small fishing fleets and, until about a month ago, this had been one of the best winters for the shrimpers for a long time. Then I watched the small, tubby shrimp boats come into Silloth (now a busy port for grain from Europe) on a full, rough tide. These men, unlike the Morecambe Bay shrimpers, boil their catch at sea and steady plumes of steam came up from their iron-cauldron boilers and, as the boats slid to their moorings, the orange nylon nets were already neatly laid on deck – accents of colour in a grey world. Today, with the sun and a blue sky there were no shrimp boats and no shrimps: the melted snow-water from the Scottish and Lake District hills has driven the shrimps to warmer waters. The other fishers of Solway, the birds, waited on the tideline as the sea went back – big flocks of oystercatchers, redshanks, dunlins and knots, and most of them were silent. Sometimes, however, the redshanks broke out into high, musical whistling very like the voice of the north wind in the marram grass.

Keswick

This is a good year for blossom, the foam of wild cherry is retreating from the valleys now but upon the fells even ancient and storm-scarred trees shine white, as white as the snow which today lies on the mountain-tops. All the garden bushes – currants, gooseberries and raspberries – are thick with flower or bud and this year, for the first time in many, the sparrows have left my cut-leafed Japanese maple untouched. They usually take the buds almost as soon as they show but perhaps this damp spring has made the difference.

Broom and gorse are yellow, sycamore is coming to flower and soon there will be apple blossom. Indeed, this is the time of year – the awakening – when I miss my bees which I had kept for so long and parted with three years ago. I still feel a surge of excitement in a good blossom year and remember the contented hum of working hives just as I remember the kindliness of many of my fellow beekeepers. It seemed to me that bees, like other creatures, take after their owners – the over-careful, perhaps nervous, ones have kittle, 'hot-footed' bees, while the happy, easy-going ones preside over quietly contented stocks. One jumpy beekeeper here kept a bottle of ammonia (much needed) in his hedge for his own and his neighbours' solace but one of the older bee-men, by contrast, went round the countryside to clover or to heather with teeming hives in his car boot and its interior humming with bees. But, as he said, he never went 'agin t' bees'; he did not (so far as I know) tell the bees of family events as beekeepers were reputed to do but he often said, 'Let t'bees tell you, go with them, not agin them.' That was, indeed, his philosophy of life – go with it, not 'agin it'.

Lake District   17 March, 1969

It is difficult at present to find any colour on the fells or in the valley and even the woods are colourless. The insignificant green shoots on the honeysuckle, the red of dogwood, the yellow-green of willow stems and the glow of the Scots pine bark have all to be looked for – but so have most things of interest and one is being conscious sometimes in the bare woods of being seen rather than seeing. The woods are quiet, too, so small sounds carry and louder ones startle; one's footsteps may be deadened on moss or leafmould but even here a human being cannot escape notice. Today, as I went through the woods, a greater spotted woodpecker who had been hammering industriously on a rotten beech put its head round the trunk and 'chacked' indignantly; four squirrels watched from the larches; six herons from a spruce and two roe-deer from the thicket. The squirrels had been interrupted in their own affairs, one eating cones at the end of a larch branch, a second digging at the foot of the tree, but the other two chased one another up, down, and around a tree trunk, chittering with excitement. The herons are deciding on nest sites and took little notice, only indulging in rather barnyard noises. But the deer were silent, so silent that it was only a slight rustle of dead beech leaves, a slight movement against the dark yew background, that showed there was anything there. The first one, small and grey, raised its head and sniffed the air, then moved leisurely up the knoll and drew attention to a second, bigger beast. They stood together for a few seconds, the smaller outlined against the larger, like a pair of paper cut-outs and there were off-white tail patches prominent.

Lake District   *31 March, 1969*

It has seemed for some time now that there are fewer otters in this district. They are certainly infrequent in their usual haunts and some of their traditional breeding places are forsaken – a mill at Cockermouth, a hollow under a road near Grasmere, and rock-holts near the head of Derwentwater are all deserted. The mill is ruined, its lade gone, and the other two places are made untenable by people and traffic. However, the recent stopping of otter-hunting in the south and the fact that it goes on here made me wonder, again, if there really are fewer otters or have they – like some Lake District dwellers – simply withdrawn to quieter places. I have walked many river-bank and lake-shore miles recently in search of otter signs. What was I looking for – not only otters but their 'seals' (pawmarks) or 'spraints' (droppings) on favourite rocks; the little green trackways otters leave on meadows between one turn of a river and the next. I saw no otters and no spraints but I found some seals and one green track, used for generations, is still in use. Last week I wandered, early one morning, down a muddy path to the river and there, below straggly hawthorns, was an otter – but it was dead. It was a fine young female, struck, it seemed, by traffic on the road above, for there was a mark on her side and bright blood oozed from her mouth on to the spring green. She lay there, totally limp, surprisingly long (almost a yard in length), her thick-based tail curved back. The black leathery webs of her paws were furled now, like chestnut buds, her coat dewed with moisture.

Keswick   28 April, 1969

Junipers grow on poor, wild ground anywhere from East
Africa to the Arctic, or so I am told, but naturally it is the
Lake District ones I know best and these present a great
diversity of shape and size. There are tall green juniper spires
rising maybe twenty feet in height; low, rock-hugging
carpets and old, lichened bushes with stems as thick as a
man's thigh. All are very much at home on the wet, acid rock
and all, locally, are called savins – why I do not know. They
are either *Juniperus communis*, or rarer and smaller *Juniperus
nana*; a cultivated sort is called *Juniperus sabina* (which sounds
a bit like savin) but this has nothing to do with the fells and I
cannot find the name savin in any of my books, old or new. I
often get told that the deer have been 'in the savins' and a
farm sold recently in this district had pieces of land called
'High Savins', 'Savin Close', and so on.

It was very wet this morning as I plodded up through the
juniper thickets from the Thirlmere Valley to Harrop Tarn; it
was the sort of rain which does not look heavy but which is
certain, eventually, to get through almost any clothing. The
path was like a waterfall; there was new snow on Helvellyn
and the clouds were low on the slopes, but it was far from
being a dismal day. Dobb Ghyll thundered in its rocks,
wrens sang in the junipers, a gay male wheatear – newly back
– sang and flew from stone to stone while kestrels 'kee-kee-
keed' on the crag. The frost has touched some of the junipers
but many are strong and green and the pin-points of this
year's flowers are showing and last year's berries (they take
two years to ripen) are green and violet-purple. I brought a
handful home, there is nothing like juniper berries to warm a
stew or a pot roast.

Keswick   12 April, 1971

I went up the fell, alone, early one morning this week while
the lower spruce wood was still in shadow but the sun was
already warm in the higher beech wood, where the thin, grey
beech trunks and the warm brown of the fallen beech leaves
make a perfect foil for the red-deer – but there are no deer to
be seen. There were round, flattened beds in the leaves where
they had lately lain and deep slots where their hooves had

sunk into the leafmould. It was very quiet and there was a sense of being watched. The character of the wood changes as it rises: spruce, alder, beech and high-level stunted larch, but nothing marks the change more than do the mosses and lichens. Liver-worts are in flower near the roadside, polytrichum and tamarisk moss make green cushions in the deciduous woods and higher up in the beck (in the black shade of the spruce) alone, three-cornered triads of *Fontanalis antipyretica* hang over the wet boulders. It seems strange to find this moss, usually associated with deep streams, in such a place – *Fontanalis antipyretica* (as its name implies) was used in Scandinavia (and maybe still is) to fireproof between stone chimneys and wooden roofs and perhaps, too, it was used at Hawkshead in Westmorland. A bill there, among old papers, is 'for re-mossing roof'. The deer had been nibbling the newest juniper shoots near the top of the fell and knocking the grey, woolly hair moss off the scree, but they were still invisible and it was dusk, and another day, before I saw some of them – four hinds, alert and very watchful.

Keswick   *8 May, 1972*

The fields round the fell farms, the in-bye fields, are gay with lambs for both this spring and last and their preceding winters were comparatively mild, so lambing has been good. New-born lambs may seem to shiver at their first arrival in the world, but almost at once they are up on their feet and feeding. They can stand a lot of cold and even bitter winds, but not cold and wet together – and fortunately this spring, so far, has been on the dry side. There are therefore few pet lambs – lambs orphaned or discarded by milkless mothers – which are a farmer's curse. Not only do pet lambs have to be bottle-fed and watched for some time, but some never integrate with the rest, like one well-known and turbulent character, Nancy, who liked her own company best and would not even go to the fell in summer, preferring the perils of the green road-verges to the freedom of the hills. Foxes, though, remain the lamb's worst enemies, but now the local hunt is only out after potential lamb-killers very early in the day. The gallery of hunt-watchers with cars is gone and only the devoted remain.

Keswick

There is often a day in mid-April when the quality of the
light and air suddenly changes, when you may look down
into some small valley and see the tops of the oaks, alders,
and birches misted over with colour or you may look up to
the snow-line on the fell and see there a deepening of colour
in the heather at its edge. On such a day, too, you might
come on a place so lost, so unpeopled, that there time slips
through your fingers like a thread of silver sand or a half-
forgotten tune. There is a small church only half a meadow
away from the river Derwent in Cumberland which, today,
had that feeling of being out of time. It was very silent and
warm there, and the air unstirring, so that the golden spread
of daffodils in the churchyard and along the river only moved
where the spring-drowsy bumble-bees blundered in and out
of their trumpets. The church, 'half as old as Christendom',
is exquisitely clean and has a Norman arch and thick
defensive walls but, to me, it is primarily a strong link
between pagan and Christian. After all it is beside the 'oak
river' (the Celtic word for oak trees is *derwen*) on what may
once – when people made their ways through thick forests
and along river-sides – have been a river-crossing even before
the Cross came here. It has ancient stones, one of which has
four symbols – a swastika, a triskele (the three legs of Man)
and another, all above a sun snake. It is said to have been part
of a cross-shaft but no one knows. The old orchard between
the church and the river is wholly grey now, each twig and
branch furred over with such a growth of lichen that they are
three times their real size. One plum tree manages a few pale
flowers, a few leaves, outside the grey mass but it seems that
the fate of the other tree is already set. One half expects to
find mistletoe in such a place but, perhaps, it is too damp, too
northerly for that?

Keswick

10 March, 1975

One of the most cheerful sights in early March is the
liveliness in and around the badger setts. The badgers are
hard at it now – cleaning out, re-digging, and in some places
dragging in clean grass bedding. There will be cubs soon but
no one will see them until, say, mid-April. The setts I visited

this morning are sheltered from the easterly wind and the sun lights them quite early, so as I went down the muddy track I could see the outline of huge heaps of new earth against the misty blue fells and the bright sky. This is steep and shaly ground but old oaks hold the banking steady and the badgers make use of the roots. There must be many unseen, underground roots for roofs and supports and two of the holes have stout oak porches and lintels. One even has a stone- and oak-slabbed side. The warm, pleasant smell of badger hung about the place but, naturally, there was not an animal to be seen. It was easy to see, however, where the night had sent them – digging out a grub-riddled stump, working on a new hole and bulldozing through the blackthorns. The badger latrines are up the fell in the edge of a spinney and one row is set almost communally along a tree root – reminiscent of a row of wooden-seated earth-closets which once adorned an outhouse at Seathwaite in Borrowdale, only perhaps the badgers' ones are neater. There were splodgy footprints on the path down the fell, both inward and outward bound. The outward looked leisurely but the homeward had hurried, perhaps run, pushing pad and pawmarks deep into the mire.

Keswick

There is a wealth of flower and blossom everywhere this year and surely last summer's sun must get the credit for some of this? Even the usually sombre spruces are having a brief time of glory – their handsome, unpollinated female flowers stand up like small scarlet Christmas candles in the crowns of the trees and even the paler, male flowers punctuate the lower branches with colour. The brisk April wind will usefully ensure a good cross-pollination since male and female flowers open at different times on different trees. The tall spruce at my gate stands at the end of a line of wild cherry trees which are a mass of tumbling white – a clear white quite different from the creamy white of the Kendal damsons adorning the Lyth Valley now. I stood there at noonday in a friend's garden on the warm side of Whitbarrow Scar looking down the valley to the sea – butterflies floated over and a cat dozed comfortably between the potato ridges. It is a peaceful place. A lot of the damsons are getting old now but will they ever be replaced? Indeed, the story of Lyth is repeated all over the Lake District valleys whether the trees are damson or plum, oak, ash, sycamore or even hazel coppice on fells and in fields – trees come to maturity, get past it, and go. What will the countryside look like in years to come? It lives now on the bounty of past generations and very little on that of the present.

Keswick   7 March, 1977

This is mostly a time for small prospects, closer views – for too often mist and cloud cut off the mountains and the sky, giving greater value to the near-at-hand. Not all days are grey, some have a mother-of-pearl sheen – a pink light through parted clouds – but even on such a day it is difficult to distinguish the swelling silver catkins on the willows from the raindrops hanging on the stems. Only the sun can turn the drops to diamonds. The silver birches outside my windows give perches – and frames – to a pair of collared doves, themselves a silvery grey flushed with pink. They are very vocal now. However, green is rising up the willow wands, the dogwoods are red and the flower buds on the elms are warm with colour – it is time, in fact, to go round the badger setts. Three weeks ago there was only moderate activity; now there is a real surge of action, especially in one lot. One hole was used all the winter and it is being cleaned out, two older ones are being vigorously excavated and a third (which has been out of use for years) is being properly and deeply dug. Every morning shows a change and it is astonishing what a badger can shift in a night, quite big roots are gnawed through and dragged out, large stones are fetched out and left to slide down the hillside but – most intriguing of all – is the variety of old badger bones in the debris. Traditionally, badgers which die of natural causes die underground and are walled in by other users of the hole.

Keswick   4 April, 1977

The intention when I went up the Newlands Valley was to have a good stretch in the Keskadale oaks – a wood of almost purely sessile oak on a precipitous slope between 1,000 and

1,500 feet up and said by some to be the remnant of a native oak forest, but the valley was at its most forbidding and still given over to winter. It was an unpropitious morning, the air was very cold and rain drifted over the fell and the climb up to the trees is a mixture of muddy, shaly scree and sliding grass tussocks moored lightly by sheep-nibbled gorse on the lower part, heather higher up. There are only a few flowers on the taller gorse, shut now and waiting for warmth to give out their vanilla sweetness. Hungry sheep crossed and re-crossed the slope all the way from the greener in-bye fields to the hard line of rock against the sky. The lower part of the wood had to suffice and its oaks are still grey, winter-budded, and even the moss looked half dead. The coming-down was worse than the going-up – not recommended – but the prospect of the valley below comforted; a yellow-pollened willow shone by the Newlands beck and a curlew called there. There is, too, an ancient clump of box well below the oaks which always intrigues me: it is a magnet for nesting birds and some of its stems are nearing twenty inches in diameter, thriving astonishingly on this acid, wind-swept hill. How did it get there – a bird-borne seed, an escape from some dwelling and was its wood ever used? Boxwood is hard, yellow and fox-smelling and used for making small objects – I have a boxwood ruler and I recall, with pleasure, an ivory-smooth box prodder used for making rugs on a neighbouring farm years ago.

Keswick   *21 April, 1977*

Green growth was strong here until a few weeks ago, the grass and the hedges seemed to be loosening from the shackles of winter and then, with little warning, the weather turned around. This was, perhaps, a 'tewit storm' – the time when, as the peewits come back to their high nesting grounds, the last fierce lash of winter strikes. The peewits were certainly there on the fell and they and the first of the curlews stood stoically, backs to the snowy wind. They waited, as we do, for better days. It was hard on the ewes and the new lambs and even the cheerful farmer who brings the milk – and not one to grumble – admits that 'it is nea good at all', and with baled hay the price it is it is no wonder that farmers worry. But even though there was a seeming pause in the year, a lot went on in a quiet way, fields were harrowed, muck spread and some ditches cleared in spite of the clarty land. I must sow grass seed, as soon as the ground is fit, on a stretch of good vegetable land to save labour and let it revert to orchard as it once was, but the real question is when to plant potatoes. Good Friday is a traditional day – but a hopeless one this year. A (well-tried?) local rule is to wait until the earth is warm enough to sit on comfortably, with no clothes or otherwise, between you and it. This, I might add, is not my method. The lack of urgency in the garden has given time to wander, time at dusk to wait and listen, until the first-wakened brown owls send their shivering calls across the fell where the badgers live and in the morning, a soft and gentle one today, to follow down the river and find the first otter tracks I have seen there for almost three years.

Keswick   *14 May, 1979*

Skiddaw in the first days of May looked grim, seeming almost to lean over the valley – an illusion given by the earlier snowfields and cornices on the top ridges with often a dusting of new snow and frost on the dark lower slopes some mornings. But Old Windebrowe sits comfortably below the breast of Latrigg (Skiddaw's Cub) and above the river Greta and its bank of trees. This is where William and Dorothy Wordsworth stayed from April until October as guests of William Calvert in 1794 – five years before their Grasmere days. Two rooms in the older end of Windebrowe are now open to the public each Wednesday afternoon from now until October, and the small entrance fee is given to the suitably named Calvert Trust – an adventure centre for the disabled at Little Crosthwaite, above Bassenthwaite Lake and also under Skiddaw. William and Dorothy came by coach to Kendal and took two days to walk to Keswick, stopping a night at Grasmere, having passed by Dove Cottage with perhaps barely a glance at the place which later was to hold so much of their lives. The year 1794 was a happy and a lively time for them, in spite of Aunt Crackenthorpe who wrote upbraiding Dorothy for 'living in an unprotected situation' and 'rambling about the country on foot', to which Dorothy replied seemingly gently but (surely?) with a hint of rebellion. Their life was simple here, their fare even more so, and the room they principally used still has its original fireplace and brass-knobbed bake-oven with pans and

35

furniture such as they might have used. The other room (until lately a harness room) has a range of treasure – original letters, books, portraits of the Lake Poets and their friends. There is a wall now across the cobbled yard from the windows which cannot have been there in 1794 but this afternoon the sun shone warmly over its top and into the little rooms. It shone too on the old, budding beeches outside, the unfurling green fingers of the horse chestnuts and the bright yellow flowers of the maples down the lane – a happy place still.

Keswick *28 May, 1979*

This is what I call cuckoo weather when the early day glitters in freshness, showers and sun together, with rain-drops on the new growth and a cuckoo calling along the fell and across the valley. A blackbird sings in the bare oak above its nest in the blackthorn. Indeed everything seemed very green this morning on the fell road, and I often wonder who lived in this straggle of buildings long ago where one house has the date 1688 over its lintel and the cottage and its bank-barn above seem even older. The plants here may give some clue to the sort of people they may have been for, though it is said that there was no witchcraft in north Cumbria (perhaps the Scots gave all the excitement that was needed?), there were certainly white witches, wise women who knew and used both pot herbs and simples. Consider the steep bank, crowned by an ancient hedge, which slopes up between the road and the fell: it has a wealth of growth, some of it modest like the sweet white violets under the thorns whose seeds were used to reduce swelling, and the green alkanet said to 'restore those of melancholy and dismal habit'. Some of it is rampant: thickets of bistort for herb puddings, nettles for broth and young greens, a froth of Sweet Cicely (anise-scented in leaves and root), and Jack in the Hedge, Sauce Alone, to eat with fell mutton. There is comfrey, too, for bruises and breaks and for its young leaves to dip in batter and fry in butter to eat with sugar – or honey. But for me the soft blue-green leaves and yellow flowers of greater celandine (*Chelidonium majus*, Greek for a swallow) are the very essence of May. It is said to flower as the swallows come, but both blossoms and birds were late this year so it is left to the untamed dog violets and the primroses on the hill to give colour to this damp, emerald morning.

Keswick   27 April, 1981

There are some farms it is impossible to go past without stopping for a crack – and who would want to? The farmer had just given extra feed to his lambing ewes as I went past the field gate this chill, sunny morning. The lambs have come quickly this last week and they and their mothers look in good fettle. One ewe, with twins born during the night, was easy in a small stone hull where the warm sun shone in; but the orchard corner opposite had a more unusual sight, a rough-faced ewe with four very small lambs a few days old. They are still tottery but 'furnishing' (filling out) and unless cold rain comes should do well. The damson blossom which overhung them is just in bloom, things are late on the fell-end. But I had really come with a piece of horse furniture which has been on a high shelf for years. It is a stout, buckled strap of thick leather with a brass plate flanked by a heart and a shield. The farmer says he thinks it's a bit long for a 'martin', 'martindale' to him, a martingale to others. It is more like a 'yam': this is a hame, part of a draught horse's collar with hooks to take chains for dragging timber, a harrow or whatever is needed. We both belong to a generation for whom draught horses were part of life and, as we talked, a tractor took a roller over the growing grass in the next field. No good for plovers, he said, remembering the horses who gave a man time to shift nests or young to the field's side. He had one good bit of news to add – last year, and this, there were and are many more curlews nesting on the marshy lands below the farm well out of harm's way.

Keswick   11 May, 1981

The air can be very cold now, the light silvery, both early and late – so overlook the cold and use the light. The banks under the oaks were bright with dog violets and wood sorrel this morning and shining with raindrops. The willow warblers and the chiffchaffs are singing again, April's blackthorn winter forgotten, and there is a grasshopper warbler in the rushy ground. The badgers had long returned to bed, doubtless extremely muddy but well filled with a night's harvest of earthworms, pignuts, and maybe an early bees' nest. But it is unwise to move off too hastily so soon in the day; if I had I might have overlooked a roe below me on a dry hummock out in the lake-marsh. It was outlined against a greening willow but its coat so nearly matched the dead sedges as to be almost invisible and, as I watched, it sank down to rest out the daylight hours. The air was even colder and a wind had got up when I went back there towards dusk, still in silver light, to see if the badgers came out. The wind roared through the tops of the oaks and even sifted through the overgrown thorns which give me cover. The night was full of small, unnameable sounds in the undergrowth and owls called up the fell, but no badger stirred. Only a bat swept – very distractingly – round my head and across my face. The smell of crushed nettles and of hedge-woundwort rose from under my feet and the scent of new, green, hawthorn leaves (only in early May?) clung in my nose until the cold was beyond doing with – time to go. The scent of the leaves was still there as I slid into sleep an hour later but then from a handful by my bed.

Keswick   *13 April, 1982*

'The people were hard at work ploughing, harrowing and sowing, lasses spreading dung – a dog barking now and again.' Such was Dorothy Wordsworth's Good Friday in 1802. It would be hard to find so busy a rural scene now but the bones of the fells remain and much of the life that the Wordsworths lived is still very fresh in the barn-museum near Dove Cottage in Grasmere Vale. I went there this sunny, spring morning and found (as I have always known) that it is not the obvious treasures like fine portraits and precious manuscripts that matter most. It is the little, unregarded things. Look carefully at a kitchen interior of a yeoman farmer's house with the grandmother, daughter and cradled child beside fire and table – is it not the everyday things of fabric, iron and wood that stick longest in the mind? Wordsworth's coat stands below a wall of portraits but there is his post-bag, his much-used sandwich box and a dark stick common to both William and Dorothy. William's wife, Mary, owned the penknife and handkerchiefs alongside. A case opposite the kitchen scene holds bones for pinning roofs, cockfighting spurs and 'Spooner's Transformation', a picture of two fighting cocks whose heads, held to the light, are of Napoleon and Wellington. In front of them is a clutch of vivid Easter eggs decorated with careful artistry by James Dixon who worked for the family for thirty-three years and helped William after his daughter Dora's death. I took some of the road back to Keswick which the Wordsworths often walked and though there are no primroses on its banks now, the pilewort (lesser celandine) shone like stars of gold as they did for Dorothy 180 years ago.

Keswick   28 March, 1983

The end of March, the start of April, and the lawn-mowers are emerging on to rather mossy lawns after one of the dampest and mildest winters for years. I do not want to start, or continue, an argument but I wish someone could tell me with any certitude how harmful, or not, moss- and weedkillers and indeed sprays are generally to the birds who feed along the lawns and elsewhere. I have noticed and commented on the declining number of small birds here for some years now. It has been said that gardens in and around towns will soon become important refuges for birds in these days of hedge and rough-land clearance. Is it true? It seems foolish to feed birds in winter and provide nest sites, and yet use perhaps doubtful products in gardens. Until about twelve years ago a whitethroat always raised broods near my nettle bed – it is still thriving – and while these birds' troubles probably lie in their wintering places, other warblers – willow, chiffchaff, and garden – are fewer, too. Even chaffinches and song thrushes are less common here; indeed, only blackbirds are 'common', though dunnocks, tits, wrens, or robins are much the same. Neither the resident sparrowhawk nor the magpies can be blamed; they have usually been about for the last five years. I have used no garden chemicals (yet) and as a reward have disgracefully lichened apple trees, and a tree-creeper to enjoy them. I came home last night in a soft, damp twilight to moths at the windows and a blackbird singing itself to sleep, just as the owls began to call in the far wood. But could we, too, come to a 'silent spring'? An old gardening book recommends lime wash for mossed trees, fine coal ash for the lawns, and 'refuse' salt for green paths. Other days, gentler ways?

Keswick   25 April, 1983

Cumbrian rivers and becks have been sources of power since Roman times for all sorts of mills and factories – woollen, cotton, and bobbin mills, forges and gunpowder works – but corn mills predominate. I came on one recently on a cold, shiny morning when the wind set the purple alder catkins bobbing and bowed the daffodils along the river and the disused race. It looked, at first sight, that little of interest could be left there, but a slow – and very cautious – exploration showed otherwise. The tall, narrow building, the wide race and two fine bays for carts in the end wall suggested a lowder mill. Lowder mills (unusual in Cumbria) had the water wheel inside and partly below ground, the stones above mounted on stout beams (the lowder) and hoppers alongside or again above. An old man joined me from the stackyard and together we went into the enveloping gloom. One room led to another, the beams were rotted and fallen, a stone was sunk by a wall, and no floor was to be trusted. The mill stopped work fifty years ago but the old man remembered it in busy times – his family have been there for 150 years. One of his cobwebbed relics was strange to me. It looked like a huge iron crochet hook mounted on a curved wooden handle. It was used for making simes (straw ropes for tying round stacks), and it took two men to make a sime. One had the instrument's end hitched to his belt on a swivel and a stack of straight straw beside him to feed through the hook, twisting it as it went while his companion moved back, twisting too, as the rope grew. Only barley is still milled here, with a small petrol engine, and it lay in a wooden scoop – silky and damp to the hands and very sweet to the nose.

Keswick   23 May, 1983

I went over Dunmail Raise today on a true May morning of flying sunshine and showers and found on the top of White

Moss Common – the old road from Grasmere to Rydal – that 'strange mountain lightness' between the valleys which Dorothy Wordsworth knew so well. I saw too, in flower, an ancient pear tree which is still growing where a cottage once stood beside the valley road. Its trunk is fissured with age but its line will go on through a young pear tree in Dorothy and William's garden at the back of Dove Cottage. It was grown lately by the keeper of the garden from a pip of that original tree. That is typical of the garden, a tilted rise of rocks, trees and plants – their 'domestic slip of mountain' – where increasingly plants are being encouraged which would have fitted into its life almost two centuries ago. It is a mixture of wild and tame. The front of the cottage has a tangle of matted green punctuated now with Honesty, London Pride and Bleeding Heart. At the side and the back there is a herb border and easterledges grow in the grass with lesser celandine leaves – William's 'bright coronet' and Dorothy's 'pilewort'. Primroses and windflowers shelter under the stones which rise up past the rockpool to the summerhouse. You look down from there to the intricate jumble of the cottage roofs and the garden door whose porch is a stone slab laden with ferns, bistort and greater celandine – *Chelidonium majus*, supposed to flower when the swallows come. I saw no swallows but thrushes, chaffinches and a solitary blackcap warbler.

Keswick

26 March, 1985

It is Lent, so there are no flowers inside the small and ancient church beside the river Derwent; nor does it need any. There is nothing now to distract the eye from its austere flowering in stone of brown, pale fawn, and near rose red. The Norman arch has all of these in its alternating blocks. The earliest slits and lancets admit very little light, but it flows in: a cold spring light searching into every clean-swept corner through the later clear-glass windows. It picks out unrelated stones like the tenth-century cross fragments by the door and the triskele stone, three-legged with strange symbols on a sill. All are older than most of this mainly Norman building. St Michael's in its peaceful countryside has been lucky in its builders, rebuilders, and craftsmen down the years and in those who care for it now. A card of Sir John Betjeman's beside a window is its best description: 'A perfect English harmony of man and nature.' That is true of the church, but it is equally so of the land outside, of the churchyard and the meadow between its wall and the river. The snowdrops were the first to come under an old beech beside the wall, followed by aconites and early fragile crocuses. They came in snow, and in the mid-March snow they faded, to be followed by daffodils. These are sadly not the wild ones of the Westmorland valleys, or, happily, the stiff modern ones, but more generally the half-double daffodils which flourish, green-tipped and uninvited, in any older garden.

Keswick 8 April, 1985

The sun had long set but the sky was still on fire with its afterglow when, one evening lately, I turned for home leaving the valley bottom in shadow. The stream ran quietly, a polished steel line where the gold of sunset could not reach. It was a still evening, too, with nothing stirring except at the furthest turn of the bank where ripples widened, joined and crossed, and a drake mallard floated down to settle for the night on an island of sedge, safe from the foxes. Nor was there any sound, no curlew voices or lapwings yet, and the stream only murmured on the stones under the bridge. The farm on the crest of the hill was sharp-cut against the flare of the cloudless sky – its jumble of roof lines, barns and gable-ends solidly blue-black. Its windbreak of firs and larches tailed away into a scribble of spaced beeches stretching north. The steep hill up past the farm was empty and not even a dog barked from the dark yard. Then, on the top of the rise the full glory of the western sky lay spread out from the Borrowdale fells to Bassenthwaite and north to Skiddaw, lighting even the smallest puddles at the roadside to burnished red-gold. The stones of the Castle Rigg circle were, by contrast, very dark and unreflecting. It had, in fact, cast off its popular, much-photographed, image and reverted to its real self – no maidens these who dance at a solstice, no knights who go down to the stream to drink on midsummer night. They were content to be The Keswick Carles, the old grey women who keep watch alone.

Keswick

There has been a lot of north wind this spring, as there often is here, and its latest breath came searchingly into every corner of the farmyard on the fell. The cobbles were dry this morning and partly swept, the lads had finished mucking out but then this is a farm which is well kept even in the miriest weather. The farmhouse sits in the centre of its buildings, barns, byres and lofts, like a hen amongst chickens. Everything was in order. Lambing is almost finished, it has been a good year with plenty of twins, a few triplets and, happily, no pet lambs in the orchard but the orchard does not lack life. Late daffodils bend in the wind and the viburnum on the house wall is full of scent. A greenfinch was busily stripping the buds from a big plum tree, leaving the damson trees to open their first flowers. There was more shelter in the valley bottom. The green catkined willows hardly stirred and the sunlight shone up the length of the beck. Waterweed fanned below on the current, the green spears of flag iris just broke the surface and only the dark, poisonous, green dropwort stood clear of the flow. The ashes are clotted with purple-brown flower buds. There are signs of occupation round the badger sett but each spring is a race – shall I have a chance to watch there or will the pushy, inquisitive cows be turned out after winter? I have won so far this year, abetted by bad weather, and an old farmer in the Lyth valley always said that nasty spells, 'cow-quakes', often came with the new grass.

Keswick

It is possible to live in these fells for a lifetime thinking that you know every hill and fold of land, each barn and farm, even in ruins, and be proved wrong. I came on a small ruinous house on a shining May morning. It was tacked on to and concealed by a newer, sounder barn whose three doors stood open showing cobbled, stone floors and ancient muck. The roof and the first floor were mostly fallen, but to judge by what remains this was no ordinary house. Its four, small south-facing windows are eyeless now but have good stone mullions, and there is nothing to stop shafts of sunlight falling into what was once the kitchen and picking out the dark cavity of a bread-oven heated with wood or peat before the baking could begin. Its round back juts out from the outer wall. A cramped dairy-pantry faces north and has stumps of beams – which have held shelves – above a cooling slab whose stone pillars remain. A massive stone staircase spirals up, nearby, rounded into the north wall leading now only into space and its stone steps lean drunkenly. No one will climb it again. Some places even in age and ruin keep their feeling of past peace and contentment, as this one does. Swallows are back in its eaves, sheep and lambs rest in its garth under old ash trees and its spring still runs green under cresses. I shall not rest until I know more of its story.

Keswick *31 March, 1986*

This brisk March air lifts the winter-tired spirits, but the day is deceitful. It has a nip in it and the blue haze over Walla Crag is not of warmth, as it looks, but of easterly cold. There are no hive bees on the wide-open violet crocuses even at noon, but there is a ripe smell of muck being spread, a sure sign of spring. The berries are mostly gone now and put to good use by roving birds; hard berries need to be eaten and voided by them for good germination, to become the solitary hollies and thorns of some high fell or wasteland. I have a favourite holly spire which stands, a lonely sentinel, in the Shoulthwaite land among rocks, brackens and bents. It has, at its back, Skiddaw and the constantly changing sky, and is not far from the road from Grasmere to Keswick. Yew Crag is above it on one hand with the Benn on the other, making a marker for ring ousels and an occasional buzzard to visit. It is also a marker for an immensely satisfying echo which bounces back and forth from crag to crag. In coaching days the drivers would stop on the nearby road and wind their horns to set the sounds ringing to the delight of their passengers. But the road is too busy now. You must approach this holly on a road which was once a short cut for the Thirlmere children on their plod to the small school high up on the fell beside the church of St John-in-the-Vale. There were joyous hollers then, especially on the homeward way. I knew many of those children in their later years.

Southwaite *7 April, 1986*

I went today, accompanied for once, to revisit two now derelict mills – one on a river with a race to catch the water and the second on a wild fell beck. It was a typical early spring day with a glitter in the air which was caught and thrown back by the remnants of snow on the fells in gullies and on slopes untouched by the sun. The river was a smooth, steely silver only breaking into true silver where it went over the weir into white water. There was a sea of fading snowdrops under the shivering alders at the roadside and only one willow showed yellow. The miller, long retired, and the last of his family who have been here for over 150 years lives alone now with only a cat for company. A fine curly-powed bull looked over the corrugated-iron door, rattling it and rolling his eyes – not exactly company? There were no daffodils there yet nor were there any at the old mill in the upper valley, only a promise of celandines where their yellow-green buds rose above the silt left by the last flood. The beck here is very different from the river, less mass perhaps but more force, bouncing down over the rocks and boulders to throw flying spray into the air and match the sun with brightness. A pair of dippers 'follow' this beck but there were none today even though the sun, in afternoon, shone full on to their chosen nesting place in the tall wall of the barn above the bridge.

Enid
J. Wilson's
COUNTRY
DIARY

Summer

Keswick

There is a very old cherry tree on the steep side of the fell; the mice keep cherry stones under its roots and the birds drink from a natural pool in its crotch, but this evening it had a very different visitor. On its bole sat a young brown owl in its first grey plumage. At human approach it swelled up to twice its real size and clicked its beak menacingly, but when this had no effect it decided to fly and took off downwards with rather the action of an inexpert ski-jumper. It was too fat to fly easily and its wings were very untried; it bumped the fence top and shot downhill, but the fields must have seemed to come up to meet it much too quickly; it crashed into the long grass and rolled over and over in a flurry of wings and soft body. When it reached the bottom it sat up and gazed uphill as if to say, 'There, I meant to do it that way'! The light was almost gone when the mother badger came out, tasted the air, and was followed by her two cubs. They are still obedient to her training and when she went hunting they watched her every movement – noses pointed, ears alert, but made no move to follow. The owls called ceaselessly in the dusk along the valley below.

Keswick

Some years ago a local cabinet-maker rescued an oak chest which was being broken up for firewood at an inn in Keswick where he was working. One end had already gone, but he took home the rest, cleaned away some layers of green paint which covered it, and brought back to life the soft shine of the oak and the delicacy of the initials on the front – 'S.E.: 1739'. Only recently his son, wondering who 'S.E.' was, and knowing that it was the custom for a bride to have a chest to hold her linen and her belongings, searched the register of the parish church of Crosthwaite and found a record of the wedding of Sarah Edmundson, of Burns, to John Gaskgarth, of Hill Top, in 1739 – both of St John's. Burns and Hill Top both lie at the end of St John's Vale, which is part of the old parish of Crosthwaite, and face each other across its shallow valley, winding stream, and marshy field, much favoured by curlews. Burns is on the main road to Penrith and is a jumble of buildings, now adorned with fresh-leaved sycamores and flowering fruit trees; buildings and trees alike looking as if they had grown together out of the ground, so oddly are they mixed. Hill Top stands alone below the rounded end of Helvellyn, but sometimes, at sunset, its flat windows are turned to gold. The parish register indicates that the young Gaskgarths went to live at Castle Rigg nearby, and here were born two daughters, then a son, who died in infancy, and then another son, James. In 1779 it mentions 'James Gaskgarth, an Inn Holder at Keswick', so perhaps it was through him that the chest first came to the inn and, after his day, lay so long in obscurity and neglect.

Keswick

The beemaster was looking back over more than sixty years of beekeeping to when, at the age of seven, he took his first swarm. 'Aye, Father was out, an' t'neighbours came an' tell't Mother that t'bees had swarmed. Ah'd nivver been flate o' bees, Ah'd always helped Father, so Ah got t'skep an' took t'bees. Father gave me 'em later and them was mi first bees. We kept 'em in skeps in them days – see here's one on t'wall.' It had a little entrance at the lower edge and a hole at the top for the bees to go up to store honey in a skep above. Wire was put between the skeps to stop the queen going up, and when autumn came the beekeeper took the heaviest skeps for honey and the lighter ones were left to winter the bees. They were fed too with sugar and water in small, handmade wooden troughs. The comb was crushed, often bees and all, and the honey left to drip. 'But Ah'd been among t'bees long afore that. Father brought some comb in, at back-end, to drip in t'dairy an' Ah couldn't leave t'smell of t'honey alone. I got an iron spoon an' helped mysen. Ah did get a few stings but Father helped me too an' t'skelping Ah got was warse than all t'stings togither!'

Keswick

Watching badgers is an occupation that calls for the patience of Job and an ability to ignore the world around; only the mouths of the sett are important and the sounds in the fern which may indicate that once more the creatures have cheated and left by a back door deep in the green fronds.

In February two badgers were about the sett on the fell and at the end of that month, or early in March, the cubs were born. Then quietness reigned. At the beginning of April a bitter east wind swept the valley and all the hole mouths, except one, were stopped by wads of fern pulled in from the inside, whether for peace for the cubs, or against the cold I cannot say.

In May the sow fetched in much fresh bedding, and one still evening a very young cub came up to sample the air after its parent had gone hunting. It was so young that human beings were not yet to be feared and it stared at the world with gentle eyes. Its ears were very round and soft, fringed with pale fur; its nose seemed more snub than its elder's. Last night it was more distrustful, but it came out in near daylight; its sleek snout and clean black and white face looked very handsome beside the two heads of gay foxgloves which grace its home; such moments repay many fruitless waits.

Keswick

A few days of warm sunshine have dried the fells and sent the becks back to their normal courses, but the water is still tawny and turbulent in the small falls and pools below the crag. In the open the sphagnum moss is showing red and yellow for autumn, but under the junipers at the beckside it is still a soft green carpet. A large ashen-grey moth with a feathery upper body and black markings, which looked like notches on its wing edges, floated down from a juniper to the dry moss at its root. Almost at once a large ant sidled up to it and, grasping the moth's hind leg, began to stroke it up and down slowly and rhythmically. This leg stroking continued for maybe thirty seconds, and then still slowly and starting at the tip the ant began to eat the moth's leg. Although the moth gave an occasional twitch it remained passive under the continued stroking and eating. When it got to the first leg joint the ant moved backwards and started on the wings. This was too much, and, with a twig, I lifted the ant, still with a piece of wing in its mouth, about an inch away. It went underground at once. I moved the moth an inch the other way, but almost immediately the ant was out again, unladen, and again attacked. This time the spell was broken, and the moth was up and away, minus a leg joint, into the dark juniper.

Keswick   12 June, 1953

At this time of the year the long hours of twilight are the most precious hours of the day. The rising trout make silver circles on the quiet river, a corncrake grates from the meadow, and every wild thing which has cause to fear the daylight is abroad and moving, but a human being must stand on the edge of a world in which he is an alien and only sometimes, very seldom, by some small sound or some movement of a creature unafraid, can be caught for a moment the feeling of belonging to the secret world, no longer an alien, but turned back in time and part of the living twilight. There are grasses which spring back where some creature has passed an instant before; the yap of a vixen from the hazels and a small shower of earth as the cubs move to her cry. The pallid moths float over the tall haygrass and after them go the gulls, no longer the noisy, common creatures of daylight but as silent and as graceful as the moths they pursue. The bats swoop along the horseshoe of water round the meadow's edge where the yellow waterlilies are opening their buds and the still water is divided from the river by a tangle of trees. At dawn, I know, a roe-deer comes to feed in this tangle and sleep in safety through the early daylight hours. The only sound now, except for the birds and the foxes, is the soft 'plunk' of a frog as it hops along the path, striking the hard surface at every hop. A footfall is too loud and a whisper would shatter the silence, so an alien must wait between the meadow and the water while the real owners of the twilight go past on their own occasions.

Cumberland 10 July, 1953

The north Cumberland coast is alive with colour and movement in July. At low tide the water lies in pools and channels through the wet and gleaming sand; the dark rocks, under which the crabs lurk, are festooned with seaweed and studded with periwinkles. To me the periwinkles taste, when boiled, extremely like salted elastic, and an old cookery book I have remarks, snobbishly, that, 'They are brought in immense quantities to London and form a considerable article of food among the lower classes . . . the animal is picked out of the shell with a pin'! Above the tideline the birds dart and whistle; the terns curve and swoop in brilliant flashes of white against the blue sky. But it is, perhaps, the butterflies and the daytime moths which give most of the life and colour to the coast. The commoner butterflies, the blues, the graylings, and the fritillaries, are there in numbers but the host of six-spot burnet moths with their astonishing red and black wings are my favourites. Their yellow cocoon-cases, mostly empty now, are stuck to the upper stems of the marram grasses and from the cocoon openings the pupa coverings emerge like little bunches of black fingers. The moths themselves are lazy creatures in the early morning and are, I am told, called the 'ten o'clock sleepers'; when the sun shines they are full of life. As they rest on the wild thyme, or the ladies' bedstraw, their clubbed, down-turned antennae give them an odd air of listening to one another – but it is easy to be fanciful about so gay an insect.

Keswick 24 June, 1954

In the last fortnight the clouds have often been low on the mountains and have clung to the heather-covered fellside above the intake, accentuating the depth of its colour and the green of the sea of bracken below. A dry-stone wall divides the heather from the bracken and from it, down through the green, runs a well-marked 'trod' used of late by a vixen as she came to a temporary earth beside a spring where her six well-grown cubs waited for her. She generally brought them something from the fell – or elsewhere – and although it was difficult to see what she brought the response was always the same, an excited rush, an almost dog-like wagging of tails, and often a fight. The six were very well matched. While they ate, or played, or fought, the vixen sat watching on a rock above the earth, and at a signal from her, which seemed often only a lowering of her head and a tenseness of her body, the whole family was gone. Now they are gone for good – able to hunt for themselves to a certain degree – and have left a very sordid mess behind them. There are feathers and bits of unfortunate hens reived from the valley below, a breastbone of a grouse from the heather, and many unrecognisable and smelly remnants. Only about a hundred yards west of the earth, in the thyme-studded turf, a family of rabbits, one of whom is jet black and very bold, has lived unmolested during the cubs' tenancy. It seems to have been left to the badgers who live lower down the fell to deal with the rabbits, which they usually do most competently.

Keswick   *30 August, 1954*

The thick green of July growth – bracken, fern, and broom – makes a haven for young foxes on the fells; but, once out of it, they become vulnerable, like the one I met at night lately in a tunnel of fir trees between the lake and the fell. The car lights picked out the green sparks of its eyes a long way ahead but it came along steadily, sniffing along the road surface and quite absorbed. It had, I am sure, never seen a car before. Young foxes, even in babyhood, have a hint of wickedness to come and this one was no exception. Its coat was still soft and pale, its eyes, ears, and black paws overlarge for its size, and its tail was not yet a brush – only a bottle brush – but the fox-look was there. It was level with the front wheels and still unconcerned when it decided to squeeze through a hole in the wall and make for the shore. The sandpipers were crying shrilly, something seemed to have disturbed them already, and when a hundred yards further on the lights caught another fox, full grown this time and watchful on the wood's edge, it was plain that this was a young family learning to hunt, with mother in charge of the proceedings.

Twenty minutes later, back on the same bit of road, another little fox was still hunting along, careless of everything about it. Indeed, the night was given over to hunting – bats swooped after moths between the trees, frogs crossed the road (perfect prey for novice foxes), and a toad sat, road-centre, waiting for any moth unfortunate or unwise enough to drift its way.

Keswick
7 July, 1955

As time goes on, a little more is understood about the circles of standing stones and the men who made them, and they are no longer called 'Doom-rings' or 'Druids' circles' but have become, simply, stone circles. Some of them, like the Castle Rigg stone circle on the ridge above Keswick, are ably looked after by national bodies. At times, especially at full moon, the stones take on again their ancient air of mystery. Although the moon sucks all the daytime colour from the earth, it gives back its own – a different – colour, and its light is soft and warm. The moon sailed at midnight in a clear sky over Helvellyn and laid dark shadows from the stones across the grass where the white clover glimmered. It showed the unevenness of the ground far better than does the sun, and it made a line of darkness round the turf rings which lie inside the stones and another along the small ridge outside the north 'gateway', but the stones themselves did not look menacing as they sometimes do, but rather like grey sheep or old grey people who had fallen asleep or been bewitched on some other moonlit night. It made the lambs uneasy: they baaed to the ewes; the curlews called once or twice; all else was silent and still as the stones.

Keswick
5 August, 1955

Last winter's frost and this summer's unusual dryness have made the mountains treacherous and it is only on close acquaintance that they reveal their full powers. I went recently to look for a rare plant which used to grow in a gully at one end of a horseshoe of jagged crags but I shall not go there again until winter has bound the rocks. The afternoon sun was directly over the head of the gully so that, looking skywards, I saw the dwarf golden-rod outlined in gold and the head of an interested sheep also aureoled in light. I was well protected at one side by a damp rock wall, but it was evident that the surface of the place was ready to move at a touch. It was littered with dying heather and rock debris so I backed out of the gully and, borrowing the sheep's ledge sweetened with alpine lady's mantle and thyme, I rested in the sun. The sun had shone all day on a ravine across the horseshoe but now it was in shadow, its rocks cooling rapidly in the northerly wind. Suddenly, with no warning, part of the ravine-side slipped and fell clear for some hundreds of feet so that it struck the opposing rocks below with a sharp crack which filled the air with lumps of stone and sent echoes flying up the organ pipes of every cleft and gully. It was odd to see that although sheep fed high up in the crags there were none in the track of the falling rock – four legs, it seems, often have more sense than two.

Keswick   *19 August, 1955*

The wild cherries do not always fulfil the promise of that surge of blossom which hangs them with snow in the spring, but this year it has been amply fulfilled, and the trees on the hill are heavy with fruit, ranging from the palest yellow-green to the darkest and ripest of black-red. The scarlets in-between show most bravely among the leaves and the birds are busy from dawn to dark. There is a bees' nest in the swollen bole of a spruce; it is a swarm which left the farm last year and has survived the winter there. The badgers have not found it yet, but they had found a nest of gold and brown bumble-bees, and what chaos remained! A few dazed bees haunted the ruins, but most had gone. The badgers had been turning over dung too to look for beetles. The old horse who lives on the hill seems to be well known to them. One was out early last evening and listened as the horse cropped towards the sett, watched him walk up on the great pile of earth at the sett mouth, ducked down as the horse snuffled and blew into the hole, and as soon as his hooves had passed over looked out again to see him go through the fern – a little later it followed along the same path across the hill.

Keswick

Warmth lingers on the fellside long after sunset, holding the scent of the gorse until the yellow faces of the tormentil are almost closed and the wild-strawberry flowers glimmer in the falling dusk. It is too soon for the badgers and one must wait. The badgers are more than wary at present; they come out very late, and who could wonder at it for this is the first spring for some years that they have gone unharmed. Daylight had almost faded, pale moths had come out of the fern and danced in spirals above it, and the owls were still before there was any movement about the place. Then, in that time without substance when the full moon has not quite gained ascendancy, when colour is all gone and the moon's own colours are not yet laid across the countryside, that movement could have been anything – or nothing. Stillness fell again and suddenly, without warning, a sharp whickering summons broke out from below the sett and almost at once another badger put its head out of the hole in answer, it seemed, to the cry. I have heard that call only once before and it is an exciting sound. Silently the animal came out and moved across the fell so that the moonlight turned its dark fur to silver and its white fur to snow; twice it paused before joining its mate and half an hour afterwards it was still away. How long will it be, I wonder, before the cubs too are out on the fell?

Keswick

The meadows in the valley are so full of flowers that, in places, the grass is almost hidden by the white dog-daisies and a host of lesser, vivid flowers. And now, before the white clover comes to its best, the first honey has been taken from the hives. Extracting it from the shallow frames is hot work but it is a most exciting moment when the clatter of the machine stops and the turning of the tap releases a stream of golden honey. The smell of it is the essence and spirit of all the early summer flowers. When the first honey comes it is time to lay the foundations of another, later harvest and peat cutting begins. It was damp on the peat-moss this afternoon, a lonely place where a solitary buzzard circles and cries and the mountain sheep call to their lambs. There are no flowers here but the yellow tormentil, although the moor-grass is soft with pollened heads and diamonded with rain. The line of the cutting goes deep into the bog and it needs a skilled hand to use the peat spade – an ancient tool with a straight blade and one flanged edge – to advantage. The oblong peat blocks are cut and laid aside to be turned, maybe many times, before they are dry enough to use. The valley and the bog seem to have little in common, but some winter's afternoon when there is honey for tea and a peat is burning on the hearth, the scent of them both will recall this July day with its wealth of meadow flowers and the lonely peat-moss in the rain.

Keswick

There is no doubt that the numbers of campers have brought many changed ways to the farms in this district. Take Champ – he is a strong young foxhound who hunts with the pack in the winter and lives, as is the custom, on a farm in the summer, where he has little to occupy his mind but sleep and food; the latter is of prime importance. He is extremely well cared for, but he likes to add a little change of his own arranging. One morning lately, I met him just after six o'clock on a road which apparently leads nowhere, and when I asked later at the farm what his business could be I was told that he seems to have an extra sense which tells him where a new camp has been pitched and which leads him in that direction. He is most agreeable to the campers, welcoming them with that expression of benign goodwill on his face which only a hound can produce and graciously accepting any offered titbit. But some time, not perhaps in the usual visiting hours, he will return and then nothing is overlooked – meat, bacon, butter, anything may disappear, but margarine is scorned. He came to the hayfield in the afternoon with a 2 lb lump of cheese, and when a neighbour looked out early next morning there, beside a haypike, was the comfortable figure of the hound and his smaller friend, the Lakeland terrier. Both dogs had spent the night camping out beside the remains of the cheese. Yet it is more than likely that Champ will win at least one prize for the best-looking hound at the local shows before the summer is out.

Roxburghshire   7 June, 1957

The borderland between England and Scotland is the traditional home of the gipsies and from it they set out to horse-trade, to barter, or just to 'travel'; many lowland farms have notices, 'No Travellers'. They are reputedly a romantic people, 'black but very bonnie', for whom the ballad says the Earl of Cassilis's lady once left her rightful lord. I saw a gipsy family lately: a man, his wife, and five children, resting at midday beside a river on the quiet Scottish hills. The sun poured down making the river glint, making gold of the buttercups and stealing the colour from a handful of fire where a pot simmered. Blue wood-smoke curled up and over the brown canvas of their cart, four piebald horses grazed quietly and the man and his wife sat on opposite sides of the fire – she upright, he half reclining. She, with her black braids and dark face, looked the better of the two; his was a more sidelong look and his foxy colouring was echoed in the baby whose over-heavy head nodded as the eldest child – a lad of ten – shifted it on his knee. The grass was littered with torn crusts and the bones of a fish – maybe a trout which last night had swum in the burn. In and out of it all swirled three wild little girls, shock-headed, barefoot, and indescribably dirty, their flying feet just missing a very small chicken which pecked at the crumbs and cheeped loudly.

Lake District

4 July, 1957

The prehistoric remains and the stone circles of the Lake District are on high ground well above the valleys, which, no doubt, so long ago were choked with a thick tangle of vegetations, and waterlogged as well. Their names – Castle Rigg, Burnmoor, Barnscar, Stockdale Moor, and the rest – echo in their endings the sort of land on which they are, and only Banniside, above Coniston, gives no indication in the way of its setting. The walk up to the place from the valley on a morning like this under the hot sun is a very steep climb but there are consolations, and today at the crest of the hill, eight hundred feet above Coniston Water, a field of white clover is in flower; its scent carried on the upland air is like a breath from a different world. The moor beyond is wild, overshadowed by the mountain – Coniston Old Man – and from it there is a clear view over the lake to the mountains and fells to the north and east. The stones lie prone on their hillock, and only a depression in the turf shows where two urns were once dug which held the bones and ashes of a woman and a child. A bog surrounds some of the hillock and its is a typical site for a stone circle – a lonely place but not untenanted. The sheep are always here, the wheatears come in summer, and today the bog is the playground of many dragonflies. Small bright blue ones dart soundlessly past, but the big, ugly, wasp-coloured ones meet and clash in twos and threes with a dry rattle of wings.

Keswick

19 July, 1957

Once upon a time a girl in a fairy story travelled far in search of happiness, and came home to find it on her own doorstep. The same sort of thing has happened here for, because of a temporary incapacity, I have forsaken the fells for the confines of my own garden and I have learnt much in the last week.

The nine chaffinches who come to, and inside, my windows are becoming more easily definable as characters, varying from the aggressive crested cock to the most shy of this year's youngsters. I had not noticed until now the little shrew mouse living in the green-slate wall below the window. It seemed at first that she was interested in the chaffinches' crumbs but apparently she prefers slugs or a few aphids for which she searches with her delicate snout held high. She is building a nest in the wall and yesterday she collected fallen quince leaves, but today she has found the dying leaves of an *Iris stylosa* and these are greatly to her liking. She tears them with vigour, tugging and uttering squeaks of excitement – or maybe squeaks in encouragement of her own efforts. She has fallen on her back several times when a leaf has parted untimely and many times the chaffinches' sudden flight has sent her in terror to her refuge.

Perhaps, at last, I shall learn, too, what creature leaves a little pile of many-coloured moths' wings each night in the corner of the stone-floored porch.

Keswick 4 July, 1958

Today when I began to cross the moor, a stretch of heather and peat hags more than a thousand feet above the lake, the misty sky was full of the happy songs of meadow pipits until – apparently from nowhere – a cuckoo appeared flying low and very hawk-like. The songs stopped abruptly; whatever associations the cuckoo had for the pipits were evidently unpleasant ones, and soon a pack of them were in pursuit. I watched from the cover of the beckside until I realised that both the cuckoo and the little birds were too engrossed in their own affairs to take any notice of me, so I moved to a knoll of deep heather, midge-infested, in the centre of the cuckoo's flight. It had, it seemed, picked a particular site for though it flew in wide circles across the moor, uttering grunting cries and trying to evade its pursuers, it always came back to the same spot. Each time it alighted the pair of pipits whose territory this was became quite frantic: they flew in its face, buffeted it with their wings, and even attacked its back with their claws. They looked very small beside it, especially when it fanned its long wings and tail and opened its beak menacingly, but they never left it alone. Only once they flopped, exhausted, to the ground and the cuckoo took an enormous hairy caterpillar from the heather, swallowing it hairs and all. Both sides were equally determined and I left them in the beginnings of a thunder shower, after two and a half hours of battle, with the issue still undecided.

Keswick

Clipping day on a fell farm is a long, hard day and yet it is a sort of holiday too. The hay must wait and the neighbouring farmers, by giving their help freely to each other, keep alive a custom as old as the fells. The clipping is all done by hand here; each man likes his own shears best, and the line of shearers astraddle the wooden benches in the sycamore's shade outside the barn are a study in method. There is old Tommy, a yearly fixture, who is very quiet and methodical, usually refusing the beer jug on its rounds. Next to him are two middle-aged men, ruddy and cheerful, clipping with style but maybe less care, their tongues seldom silent. Two youngsters work and listen, and beyond them are older men again, one as gnarled as an old boot, but all alike enjoying the day – and the hospitality. There are changes as the day goes on but some of the old men work all day; so does the man who stacks the rolled fleeces in the barn and the farmer who puts his mark on each shorn sheep.

The work over, it seems very quiet as the colours fade at evening on the fell and the white sheep and woolly lambs fan out across the fields and the shearers retire to the long room above the yard to polish off the last meal for the day – home-cured ham, mountains of currant pastry and hot, sweet tea.

Orthwaite

This is not a part of the country rich in Roman remains, the mountains have always been too wild for that, and what there are have been little disturbed. Time may alter that but in the meantime the country folk call many things 'Roman'; it is a term one must interpret for oneself. There is a 'Roman' bridge, probably a pack-horse bridge of no great age, over a mountain stream on the seaward side of the fells, and there is a strange place called the Roman camp near a reedy lake in the hills. Today the recent rain had already made the grass greener after the drought on the steep bank and ditch of the earthwork, an oblong about eighty by a hundred yards, and there were wild purple pansies, yellow tormentil, and a few blue harebells in the sheep-bitten turf. It is a lonely place and no one is quite sure what it was, but it was most probably a medieval garth, of which there are many in the hills. There is, however, no doubt at all about it, or its use, in the mind of the old woman who first told me about its existence. She calls it the Romans' dancing ground. She has never explained, nor have I asked, who these Romans were. They are for her, it seems, a mysterious people, most difficult to pin down – a mixture of gipsies and, perhaps, fairies – but the one thing that is certain to her is that this green level by the tarn is theirs and theirs alone. Could there be a grain of reason in her fantasy? Just over the hill there is an undoubted Roman signal station.

Keswick   15 June, 1960

The twilight lingers at this time of year, indeed some nights seem to be scarcely dark at all, but there is a time – long after sunset – when the light changes and with it the whole aspect of the valley. The colours of the hills deepen, the fields look almost silver as the evening wind goes over them, swaying the uncut haygrass and making even the dog-daisies bow their heads. The scent of the honeysuckle and the wild roses thickens and the moths come out. It is an anxious time for the birds: foxes, stoats, and even the farm cats come out to hunt, so the voices of the curlews and the peewits take on an added urgency.

A green lane, buried in its hedges, crosses the valley here and at one side of it there is an old ash tree where the white owls sometimes nest. It looked deserted this evening; there were no droppings, and no signs of tenancy, so it was rather a surprise when, having climbed to the first crotch, I heard something which sounded rather like very small climbing boots going up the trunk inside and a large white owl burst out of the hole just above my head. Deep in the tree, on an almost peat-like floor, were two unhatched eggs and three very young owls. They were quite naked; one had been overset by its parent's hurried exit, the heads of all three bobbled weakly and the sound they made was scarcely audible. I left quickly and watched from the hedge down the lane to see the owl come back, within ten minutes, as white and as silent as the moths.

Morecambe Bay

These now lonely sands were busy places at ebbtide before
the turnpike road was opened in 1820 and the railway in
1857, for they carried the main traffic to the Lake District and
the north-west on foot, on horseback, and later with coaches.
It was often a perilous crossing and now they are deserted,
left to thousands of sea-birds and the few men who get their
living from the sea. The quality of the light here, today, is
quite different from the light on land. The nearer shore is
silvered with sea thrift, the hills across the estuary are
patterned with small fields – yellow where the hay is cut,
green where roots and corn are ripening – and behind them
rise the mountains of Westmorland like an immense blue
backcloth. The heat on the wet sand makes everything unreal
and insubstantial. Stakes, taller than a man, which march out
towards the tide float on a mirage of water where none is,
and the ruined castle on Piel Island across the bay seems to
shift and hover. The shrimping carts are coming home, and
at first they too appear to float until the tall wheels and stocky
horses materialise. There is a man riding on each cart and a
long net on a frame – they are dragged behind the cart for
shrimping – laid lengthwise, brown and orange, beside him.
The horses are reluctant to stop, and who would blame them
after long hours on the sands, and as soon as they have passed
the oystercatchers settle again, crying, on the sandbanks, and
doze in the sun.

Keswick

The heavy green of late summer seems to have drowned this
valley and taken much of its colour, but the crooked grass-
grown lane where the barn owls nest in a rotten ash tree is
still full of flowers – purple betony, pale meadowsweet, and
tall campanulas. The weather has been hard on the young
barn owls; four of them were hatched about 13 June, but two
of them died about a fortnight later, killed, I think, by the
sudden change in the weather and the cold rain which
followed; after all they were still in their baby-down, and
while two could get some shelter at one side of the tree trunk,
two must have been very much out in the cold. However,
after a struggle, the remaining two forged ahead – no doubt

getting double rations – and could soon produce a wonderfully menacing sound like two small kettles coming to the boil. They have kept their own characteristics throughout: the smaller one always turned its back and hid its face in the ash trunk, the bigger one squared up boldly and hissed much more loudly. The night before last the shy one still hid its face, but the other sat back on its small rear, fixed me with an unwinking gaze, and struck out with its claws, swaying like a prize fighter from side to side. This afternoon they have flown at last, leaving the nest hole surprisingly clean with only a little white down clinging to the rough bark to show that any owls ever lived there.

Lake District 8 May, 1961

One evening lately the sun set in a clear sky leaving a glow in the west over the darkening line of the fells. There are few places, I think, where the changing colours of sunset can be better seen than from a slight rise near the head of Derwentwater. The colours of the sky on a fine night such as this are reflected along the full length of the lake in ribbons of shifting gold and yellow, rippling with the movement of the water. The small pools in the marsh, the inlets, and the river, however, reflect only the blue of the night sky and the marsh itself is dark and almost featureless except where bare ashes raise antlered heads against the sky. Though it is dark the marsh is far from silent; these nights of moonlight and the time of year have stirred many creatures into restlessness. Curlews call near the lake, the brown owls make a strange mixture of noises and – just once – a vixen calls her cubs far up in the rocks. It is the snipe, however, who really throng the marsh; they call one another, chicka-chickarr, across the swampy level and drum, supposedly with their tail feathers, invisible in the high air, with what to me is one of the strangest and most haunting noises I ever hear. In whatever way this increasing or fading murmur is made – and I could swear it sometimes comes from the ground – it is so oddly thrown that sometimes it seems to be under one's feet and sometimes very far away.

Lake District

2 June, 1961

The floor is being renewed in the big barn. It is quite rotten
with age and worn, indeed some of it collapsed in the winter
under the hay. This morning each board which came up –
broad, long boards which look as if they had been there for
hundreds of years – sent dust flying in the sunlight up to the
cobwebbed ceiling and down into the cow-byres and the
stalls below. There are small calves in the stalls, seemingly
unconcerned with the noise and the new daylight. Their
mangers and hayracks and the green slate divisions between
the stalls look, too, as if they were very, very old. Often the
travelling craftsmen who built these places left their own
marks, an initial or a date or both, on their work, but who
can explain VIIII for this part of the barn? It has seen lively
times as well as workaday ones: fifty years and more ago it
was used for dancing; people came from far and near,
including two fiddlers. Home-cured hams had been boiled in
the sett-pot, supper was laid on in the farm kitchen, and coats
left upstairs. Calico had been stretched round the lower part
of the barn walls to protect the girls' dresses and everyone
was very merry. Indeed, some, 'merry' in their own
particular way, found the little steps down into the haymew
very convenient – it was a short, soft tumble down them to
sleep it off in the hay.

Lake District

1 June, 1962

I was coming along a road here one evening this week just
after sunset, when the light was beginning to change, and
saw, to my great astonishment, three red deer moving round
a knoll beside the road. These are truly wild deer, who have
probably seldom seen traffic by daylight close at hand, and
would flee from man. They were well suited to the dead-
bracken background, for they have almost lost their winter
grey coats and put on summer's red.

Now, in the dusk, they were still nervous, the hinds
amazingly quick to dip their heads, snatch a mouthful of
grass, and raise them again, flicking their ears and sniffing the
air. The stag stayed quietly beneath a green hawthorn just
over the wall (it had taken me a long time to get into that
position) and close enough for me to see his newly springing

this year's antlers still in velvet, a covering of skin, blood vessels, and hair which will be rubbed off on some unfortunate tree.

Each time a car approached I turned gently from the deer to gaze intently at the fell opposite; this strategy worked well and it was most amusing and rewarding to see the interest created, the turned heads and craned necks, for not everyone in this district is to be trusted with deer. Indeed, eventually even the stag seemed to be breathing down my neck and looking at the fell, until a lorry shattered the peace. It shook the stone wall, the deer, and me; and when I turned again, it was to an empty landscape, not a deer in sight. Even when I crept over the knoll there was nothing to see but the evening star high up and a woodcock roding over the trees.

Keswick   24 August, 1962

Bat-light, owl-light, moth-light – what should one call the first onset of darkness when the fells are no longer visible across the lake and the smell of white jasmine and night-scented stock begins to flow across the garden? Here it is cat-light, too, for it is then that the kitten changes from his daylight self and his real nature comes to the surface.

I did not intend to have a cat, there are too many birds in my garden, but this kitten, an orphan whose owner was forced to part with him and had nowhere else to send him, is fast becoming part of the place. He is still very young, only a few months old. He plays a lot and sleeps a lot, too, as young things must; but at twilight he settles on a boulder outside the door, immobile but alert, paws under chest, surveying his small world. Let a moth or even a daddy-long-legs go by and he is off in a series of stalks, leaps and pounces. He can twist in a jump in mid-air, his body and over-long tail a flying curve, his paws separate, and widely spread. When the quarry is caught it is carried back to the boulder or the step and eaten noisily and with evident relish – indeed, one almost expects him to rustle when picked up so full of wings must he be. There are other hunters, too, in the twilight: the bats come early from the eaves, the spiders – one of which is huge, grey, and almost iridescent – wait in their webs in the jasmine and all the time the brown owls hoot softly in the trees below the garden.

Keswick

It is hard to believe, now that the rain has come, that that
blistering day last week on the Lancashire coast ever
happened. Indeed, even at the time, it had a dream-like
unreality created by the sun, which burned down from an
empty sky on the huge dunes, the silence, and the almost
complete lack of life. There had been no wind to disturb the
sand and a multiplicity of tracks showed what had gone on in
the night. Sea birds had left a few prints, but there were
many lace-like patterns made by mice and lizards and one
broad and well-defined track of a snake which was visible
from quite a distance. It disappeared underground in a patch
of marram grass. These young dunes near the sea are being
gradually settled and bound together by marram grass,
armoured blue sea-holly, and sea bindweed whose pink
trumpets rest on the sand. Behind the dunes are dry 'slacks',
and for anyone used only to finding the perfect white flowers
of grass-of-Parnassus growing in mountain bogs it is very
strange to find it poking up strongly and bushily through the
grey dwarf willow. With it hang the lovely cream bells,
red-stamened, of wintergreen (*Pyrola rotundifolia*, sub-species
maritima, which only grows in Britain in Lancashire and
Flint). Most of the rarer orchids were over, but a few
magnificent spikes of marsh helleborine (the only British
orchid with purple-brown and white flowers) bloomed on in
the taller willows. There were hundreds of butterflies, too, of
several sorts, including the common blue – a misnomer
nowadays if ever there was one.

Cumberland

It was not actually raining this afternoon but there was rain in
the air. The clouds were low on the fells, the ground sodden
and although the blue harebells and yellow tormentil kept up
a show of colour the whole feeling of the valley was of damp
greenness. There is a lot of water in the stream and though
the wind ruffled its surface coldly there was a patch of calm
on the upper side of the humpbacked stone bridge which
carries the track across the valley, and in it lay a trout, nose
towards the flow, swaying lazily like the waterweed beside
it. There were swallows everywhere, some whipped under

the stone humpback and up the water, but the majority sat, twittering, on the power cables above. Yes, electricity has come to the valley but in one farm, at least, it has made little difference. This afternoon, summer or no, there was a fire in the kitchen hearth, a black kettle rested on the hob. The range, much used, shone with black lead and the electric cooker beside it looked an interloper and is obviously not accepted into the family yet. 'T'shelves in t'oven is too narrow, there's nobbut room for two loaves side b'side. One ring on t' top is for t' kettle, an' t'other's for t' taties – but t' third'un is no good for owt – fire's handier, any road.' Let no one imagine, however, that this is a place behind the times; it is just that time means little here. There is plenty of it, and that plenty brings an ease of spirit and a kindliness far outweighing other things.

Lake District   27 May, 1964

Tonight this high moorland on the mountain's flank and the sky above it are very much part of one another. The rolling curve of the moor and the bowl of the sky above are joined and accentuated by a long plume of soft grey cloud fanning out from the red and gold of sunset – driven outwards, perhaps, by some freak of the upper air. I came to this place to watch a pair of short-eared owls who are nesting in the heather but there is much else, too, to see. Drifts of bog cotton are just beginning to show white and there are black peat-hags and treacherous green sphagnum bogs where bog rosemary grows. This plant, whose delicate pink bells turn down over pointed green leaves, grows rarer as more bogs are drained and land reclaimed.

The male short-ear quarters the heather in curving sweeps, sometimes towering up to plummet down with the air audible in his wings. He gives a sharp wing-clap, under-body, at the foot of his stoop before rising again, but it is a nasty feeling to have an angry owl directly overhead and I almost trod on a nest as a curlew rose from my feet leaving four eggs just chipping. A faint 'cheep' came from one of them.

Always one's eyes are drawn back to the blue outline of the western fells, the sunset beyond, and to a glimmer in the east where the moon is coming up. At first trails of vapour, left

68

by the hot day, veil the moon's face, but at last it sails in a clear sky and the moor sinks to sleep. The many bird voices are stilled and the sweet smell of moor-grass and warm ground lies on the air.

Lake District   *7 September, 1964*

The farm kitchen is very unlike itself these warm September evenings with the household god of the kitchen fire unlit in the grate. It takes a long time for everyone to come in; the young swallows have stopped twittering under the eaves and the bats are swooping against the red sunset before the farmer settles himself in his corner, shedding his clogs and wriggling his stockinged toes peacefully. It has, he says, been a good year for grass – enough rain, enough sun – but the 'early' taties were a feckless lot. The ground was too cold then. Some young fox cubs (would they, I wonder, be the ones seen learning to hunt by the lake shore a month ago?) have been in one of the hen houses, killing thirteen hens and leaving the rest silly with fear. This is the typical senseless killing of cubs learning their job and is bad to bide.

It seems a far cry from fox cubs to village policemen, but evening talk is like that, many-sided. Policemen come and go too much these days and never become part of the valley as old Tom did. Everyone here remembers him – a huge, red-faced man who would surge slowly into the pub at closing-time on a Saturday night and say, 'You young lads get off to t' dance now,' and, when they had gone, 'You old beggars can stop on a bit.' He would tell the girls after the dance to get their bicycles (lightless) down the road 'before I come out', and such was his standing that even the day his own bike frame collapsed under him, just outside the reading room, no one laughed on the spot – but they still remember, with joy.

Keswick

Apple-blossom time makes me miss my bees. I sold them a
month ago and with them seem to have gone sixteen happy
years. Beekeepers do not remember the wet years when
honey was scarce and the bees hard to maintain or the
thundery summer evenings when the bees' tempers were (to
put it mildly) frayed. One does not dwell on the back-
breaking task of extracting honey in a hot, embattled
kitchen, with all windows and doors closed against a horde
of bees outside who have smelt honey and determine to get in
or, on the cold, blowy winter nights when – for no known
reason – it seems imperative to go and see that all is well in
the apiary. Twice in my beekeeping years I have done that
and found hive roofs blown off, or hives tilted by a gale. One
remembers, rather, the hum of a contented hive at evening
when the nectar flow – apple, clover, heather or whatever it
may be – is good and the scent of it lies even on the air
outside the hive and one recalls, too, many other beekeepers
– living and dead – for I still maintain that good beekeepers
are (like fishermen) a different sort of people, slow, very
patient, and often gentle, with a humour of their own. One
old man, now gone, who had kept bees for almost eighty
years, spoke of his bees always as people and when they were
getting what most people would call really nasty would only
allow that they were a 'laal bit cottered'. He taught me a lot
about life, too, as well as bees, 'You can't,' he used to say,
'go against nature, only with her.' I have kept an empty hive
and if times get easier, maybe next year, I still may watch my
own bees on my apple blossom.

Keswick

It is obvious that the good old days were not good for
everyone; but there was a sort of contentment in the
countryside which still lingers, and with it a wealth of stories
about people and places which, unless someone records them
soon, will have gone for ever. The road from Keswick to
Grasmere is lined with history, not the sort which left the
problematical grave of King Dunmail on the Raise or even
the stone on which Wordsworth and his friends scratched
their initials, but the everyday, ordinary sort.

Now that this road is being widened the highway

authority have several small problems on their hands. They are going to move the Four Mile Stone, which marks the limit of a dissenting minister's approach to Keswick during the time of religious schism, to a new site; but there is another stone quite near it which is almost as interesting and almost unknown. This is the Echo Stone, part of the roadside wall between Yew Crag and Shoulthwaite Moss, where stage coaches and later ordinary coaches used to draw up so that the drivers with their coach horns could astound their passengers with repetitions of the echo bouncing across the valley. It was all part of the trip. I went there lately on a lovely midsummer morning with a ring ousel calling up beyond Yew Crag. It was useless shouting, the cars shot past with unnerving regularity, but a sharp handclap went back and forth beautifully, scaring a buzzard out of the crag.

Keswick　　　　　　　　　　　*23 August, 1965*

I found an old, grass-grown road last week which I did not know existed although I must have come very close to it scores of times before. It started across three big slate slabs sunk in boggy ground and went on past a hollow in the fellside, which looked as if it had been used to house animals long ago, and up past some rocks to lose itself on a green level fading into bog. These old roads are typical of this district, and their uses are not always clear, but it was not curiosity only which made me follow it: I was collecting rowanberries.

Part of the road goes through a thicket of spear thistles loud, in today's brief warmth, with bumble-bees. Indeed, the flowering thistles had created a small world of their own for foraging bees, hoverflies, butterflies, and many identical, stubby brown moths with so fast a wingbeat as to be almost invisible in sunlight; and there were big, green grasshoppers everywhere 'singing' devotedly with the true voice of summer. There are birch trees, more rowans and some scraggy pines where the road peters out in the bog, and in these pines a kestrel has two young ones who cry continually for food. She only visited them once while I was there and then the noise stilled, leaving the place very quiet. It was not, however, a dead quietness but rather a breathing, living one, for all about – unseen, unheard – was the presence of the red-deer.

Lake District

Watching badgers (or, more truthfully, watching for badgers because to know that badgers are in a sett is no guarantee of seeing them) is one of the most uncomfortable, time-consuming and sometimes fruitless occupations anyone could devise. Last night's gnat bites emphasise this all too persistently. Why, then, do it? Well – it is rather like fishing or beekeeping, the rewards can outweigh all discomforts and disappointments. One needs luck, too, as well as experience, like meeting four young badgers by chance as I did on one of the few warm May evenings recently when the world, after sunset, seemed to be breathing and expanding with a life of its own. The voices of grasshopper warblers reeling in the sedges and a woodcock riding overhead almost distracted my attention from a flicker of movement behind strands of honeysuckle on a shelf of earth above me, and there they were, four little badgers as oblivious of me as I had been of them until a few seconds before – and so they remained for almost half an hour. This was obviously a very new world for them and, to judge from their small size and their innocence, it was astonishing that their mother had allowed them out at all. Their round baby bodies were almost pinkish-grey in colour, tailed by ridiculous stumps and topped by small black ears, white-edged, and already the shining black and white badger face-blazon. They stayed close to the sett mouth, moving very gently, shoving a little at times but not, as yet, playing. One dug, experimentally, in the earth and dislodged a stone which bounced down, loud in the quietness, and this riveted all four with interest but none was afraid. Indeed, they were completely confident until a pair of late whooper swans flew in, barking sharply to one another and, in a flash, there were no badgers at all – nor have I seen them since.

Keswick

The Moot Hall in Keswick market square was once a courthouse; it is built of stone, whitewashed and trimmed with black paint, and is curious rather than beautiful. It is not at all old and is not used very much these days, but on Saturday a mixed lot of stalls occupy the ground floor which was once reserved for a butter market. The other stalls, then, were out in the square. I well remember, as a child, waiting rather impatiently while my grandmother (an imposing figure in black) slowly tasted the various butters. She always seemed to buy her butter from the same woman but the tasting ritual was always gone through and I remember, too, how good the butter looked spread out on its white cloths or – less usually – green leaves. Green leaves – my mind took a somersault backwards to those days when my eye caught a clump of plants in the turn of a farmhouse wall beyond Skiddaw this afternoon. The leaves looked, at a quick glance, like big dockens, but a proper look showed them to be monks' rhubarb (*Rumex alpinus*), a plant which is quite rare now even here in the north, where its cool, heart-shaped leaves were used to wrap individual pounds of butter, hence its local names of 'butter docken' and 'butter leaves'.

The farmer's wife who owns the plant says she has only lived there twenty-eight years and has never used it, but people sometimes ask what it is and she added that there is another clump a few miles away. Hers is, however, the one named, I think, in an old Cumberland flora as growing there in 1845. With it then grew masterwort, an equally unusual plant, and though I saw no masterwort today I shall go back – there is much to see (and to talk about) in that quiet, pleasant place.

Keswick

27 June, 1966

Last night, if one can call these brief spells of midsummer half-dark night, I waited hoping to hear the nightjars on a ferny hillside to the south of the Lake District. It is six years since I heard them there and I wondered if they, as well as the ones near here, would have gone – seemingly for ever. Nightjars, like badgers, are creatures of the dusk and, like them too, are unpredictable. Wind, weather, warmth, and even the brightness of the sky can affect their waking and how much they sing if the nightjar's spinning, continuous churring can be classed as 'song'. The sky was very light last night at ten o'clock and the evening still, so still that the fall of a dead holly leaf sounded loud and a woodcock's chirrup was audible a quarter of a mile away. The daytime birds were late to settle and a far-away hay-machine added an obbligato to their sleepy voices; indeed all the sounds and smells of summer were there which have gone from more-used places. The heavy scent of elderflowers lay in warm dips in the bracken, the opening honeysuckle was fainter, and the wild roses – glimmering in the dusk – even almost scentless. The birds fell silent and the crescent of the new moon slipped down towards the hilltop but still no nightjar sang.

I joined the farmer, a lonely man, who was leaning on his garden fence, three small pups at his feet, and only too glad to share the evening peace. There are, he says, at least seven nightjars on the fell this year, and as he talked the churring ('tuning-up', he calls it) began, rising and falling on the air. It is a sound one never forgets, more part, to me, of midsummer than even the wild roses or the milk-like warmth of evening air. The nightjars singing, he says, predicts fine weather for the day to follow, and today it is half sun, half rain.

Keswick

26 June, 1967

I have always felt that people who live in the country and go to bed – or get up – at conventional hours miss more than they know, and this last week has, for me, proved this again. After all, it can often happen that full moon and the summer solstice come together. Five o'clock is almost too late to get the best of the morning and by that time, one day lately, the sun was up in a clear sky, touching the ridge where the stone circle stands but leaving the misty Naddle Valley in shadow below. All the western side of Helvellyn was in shade, too, except where the sun struck the rocks of Brown Cove, turning them strangely pink. Raven Crag on the other side of Thirlmere caught the light early, rearing up as it does about a thousand feet above the lake. Its ledges (inaccessible even to grazing sheep) were vivid with new grass and tumbling bushes, but the sunlight travelled only slowly to the oak woods at its foot. It was cold here, but not too cold for the birds – black and white pied flycatchers, tail-flirting redstarts, and wood warblers as green as the leaves which partly hid, partly showed, their movements – to sing with a vigour and freshness only the early morning brings. Even before the light reached the lake there were silver circles on it where rising fish broke its calm surface. How different, though, is the same place at the other end of the day when Raven Crag blocks out some of the east light of the long-set sun and the moon, and one attendant star breaks clear of the clouds over the gap of Dunmail Raise. No birds sing now, no fish rise, the lake is in constant flowing movement, breaking and twisting the path of moon-silver along its length, throwing glints of light this way and that. Surely outward serenity could know no equal to its presence in this quiet place.

Walney Island 10 July, 1967

Walney Island, a curving stretch of flat and seemingly undistinguished land, lies off Barrow-in-Furness and it would be difficult to find two places more in contrast than the changing shipyards, whose cranes edge the deep-water channel, and the lonely nature reserve over the water. This reserve is managed jointly by the Lake District Naturalists' Trust and the Lancashire Trust and recently the farmers invited its members to look at the place before this year's broods of birds are on the wing. It was evident that most of the humans enjoyed the birds, but whether the feeling was reciprocated is doubtful. Some of the herring gulls – there are about forty thousand herring and black backs here – were quite aggressive, but most of them contented themselves with being noisy, and the noise (as well as sometimes the smell) was impressive. So many gulls produce the same effect as a very large hen-run, very free range. The smallest gulls stayed in their nests or hid, head foremost, in the nearest marram or ragwort, but most were mobile and all were still downy, grey and black patterned. Parties of shelduck chicks, out now from their rabbit-hole homes, were being shepherded by responsible elders in ones or twos, and a large flock of eider chicks (this is their most southerly breeding ground in Britain), similarly guarded, paddled out across the wet sand towards the old ruined pier of Foudrye, which still guards the channel.

Walney has flowers, as well as birds. There are brilliant blue spikes of viper's bugloss, the grey-green plants of horned poppy have yellow flowers now, and there are patches of scarlet pimpernel with sinister, grey-flowered henbane and purple nightshade – and, over it all, birds, flowers, shingle, sand and grass, was a whisper of wind, showers of quick rain, and gleams of sun.

Keswick   27 May, 1968

If one rises early enough these cold May mornings it is possible to catch the world half-asleep – or so it seems – on the bare, east-facing mountain flank. The early sun touches the isolated sycamores on the ridge and turns their new leaves to green-gold; it lays a glint of gold over the capsules of polytrichum moss, and lights the budding cotton-grass to silver. This is the haunt of snipe and hawks, a number of larks and wheatears and – just now – some very vocal cuckoos as well as an upsurge of voles. These last have attracted short-eared owls and, as I went up the moor this morning and saw the hunting farm cats making trails in the dew, I was struck again by the likeness between cats and owls – both excellent creatures. The first short-ear I came on was motionless on a fence post, more extension of post it seemed than bird, and it glared fixedly with fierce yellow eyes before taking wing. Once on the wing it sailed high over the heather, raised its long wings vertically over its back to give an audible clap, and then began hunting. Its eventual slip sideways on the air, its pounce in the grass, and its raised, round face clutching a vole was very cat-like and so, too, is its liking for privacy.

Keswick

There is rain again on the fells after some weeks of perfect, settled weather and very welcome it is, too. Drought does not seem right in the Lake District. Some of the crags are dangerous, rocks fall without warning and it is only the bracken which has thriven; its deep green is startling against the bleached grass of the fell slopes. Bracken is a pest here, it has spread like a flood in this century and even in the last years it has taken over much good grazing land. It is cut on some fell farms for bedding but I am told that it should be well rained on before storing to remove its pollen, which is poisonous to cattle. This is almost the last remaining use of bracken and some farms still have massive wooden sledges – iron runnered – for bringing down the bracken. Bracken was not always regarded solely as a pest, indeed some northern manor-courts safeguarded it, and at Cartmel in Furness in the seventeenth century a day was set aside – Bracken Day – before which no one could shear it for thatch or mow it for bedding. One can read, too, that at Millom (south Cumberland) in the next century, land was leased to bracken-burners at five pounds for the first two years and less for subsequent ones. The owner found housing and food for the bracken-burner's horse but – as well as the money payment – he got a share of the best ashes. No doubt there is a lot of phosphate in bracken-ash but whether it all went on the land or whether some was used in soap-making no one seems to know now. The name Ashburner, once common in Grasmere, is said to belong to this occupation. The bracken thrives this year but so, too, does the heather and this morning its opening, soft purple, is lit by gleams of sun.

Keswick

How should one say 'goodbye' to summer? Never, at least here, with sadness; each season has much of the next in it and each its joys. It seemed especially so on the fell early this morning after sun-up, but long before the dew had dried from the moor-grass. Blue haze partly hid the mountains, shreds of cloud hung in the gullies, but though it was early the honey bees were already working on the heather. It is many years since the heather here has been so fine, so glowing with colour, and its purple acres on the fells are now at their best. In the hollows even so soon in the day, one is rather in a wash of warm, heather-scented air, murmurous with bees. I found a few flowers of grass-of-Parnassus, white green-streaked and too frail-seeming for a mountain plant – but these were tight buds, too, so it is not autumn yet.

The sheep and their lambs grazed peacefully and though a little while ago this year's white lambs made their mothers look dingy and raggedy, the sheep are shorn now and, with newly sprung fleeces, they outshine the lambs. One lamb, playing and jumping alone along the beckside, disappeared from sight for a time and came up behind a family of grouse. It bounced in and out of the birds, tossing its head, but they – unconcerned and amicable – went on feeding on the heather shoots. Only the older cock bird was wary and later as I walked to the covey up they flew – eight of them, a young brood and immature – and he cursed me roundly. Grouse are alleged to say, 'Go back, go back, get to blazes out of here, and stop out.' Lambs and people are different, it seems.

Keswick   7 July, 1969

The long midsummer nights and the nights of full moon came together this year, but seldom has the sky been really clear here. One day last week the rain died out at dawn but mist lay on the fells. The air was soft, warm, and very damp. There was little wind and even towards midnight it was not dark, although the moon was hidden. The track down to the lake-marsh and the marsh itself was alive with scent and sound. Mallard stirred and quacked sleepily out on the lake, curlew and snipe kept up a constant calling along the reedy wastes, and grasshopper warblers whirred ceaselessly in the reeds. The air rustled in the tall leaves of the flag irises and along the haygrass and shifted the silver ribbon of the river, turning it light, then dark. There was no sign of the badgers and no otter moved up or down the water while I watched, but mud, water, sedges, elderflowers, dog-roses, and honeysuckle all gave their own peculiar scents to merge and separate and become part of the night's quality. The half-light left only a suggestion of yellow on the flag flowers, the foxgloves' red was dimmed, and the red campions were almost as pale as the moths – fast-flying but seeming motionless – who hung over them. One suddenly realised that this is the world as the animals know it – almost wholly white, grey, and half-black. Grey leaves, white elders, and white dog-roses – no pink for them – but the pools of darkness which, for us, hide so much, to them are not dark at all. The midsummer scents, almost overwhelmingly rich to us, are different too for them; they may not care about the sweetness of rose or honeysuckle but they must note the bitter scent of man and the scents of their own kind – those are real concerns.

Keswick   *1 September, 1969*

Threlkeld Sheep Dog Trials, until a few years ago, marked the end of summer for those who lived here more surely than the swallows gathering on the wires, the yellowing of the bracken, or any other sign of autumn. They were held then in mid-September (at least a fortnight later than now) and as well as the trials there was a hound trial and a show of foxhounds. Threlkeld was then the gathering-in of the Blencathra foxhounds and, at the end of the dog day, the pack went happily back to the kennels on the flank of Blencathra instead of separating to the farms where they had summered at ease. That is all changed now. I was up at the kennels this morning, the huntsman is cutting bracken for the dogs' winter bedding and, as yet, not all the dogs are in residence, but as we talked they broke out into that wild, blood-exciting music only hounds can make. It shows, the huntsman says, that they are ready for work, and the dogs who are here have come back of their own accord, all on their own, they know the time of the year. Two puppies frolicked round our feet, falling over one another and splashing in the puddles, but when they rushed off to the wire to paw at their elders and relatives it was possible to see in them the hard lines of the dogs to come. This is, indeed, a hard pack, working only on foot, over some of the hardest land in Britain, and many of the hounds are descendants of the 'Keswick pack' the *Sporting Magazine* described in 1828 as being dogs 'as fierce as a tiger, as long as a hayband, but with an amicable cast of features like the Chancellor of the Exchequer'. They are no different now.

Keswick

There will be no gooseberry or young-rook pies for Whit this year, although both were once peculiar to Whitsuntide here – it is quite an early Whit and a late spring. The gooseberries, well visited by honey bees, are still only small, and the young rooks are (mostly) just fledged. One wonders how much longer some of the old traditional recipes and cures will survive, but it is astonishing how many do – in a quiet way. An old woman told me when my son was small that he would be difficult to rear; he had an ivy mark (a little blue vein on the bridge of his nose) and she was quite right. She added that it would be wise to bury a jar of cream in the garden ready to dig up and lay on his vaccination mark if it gave trouble. I did not do so, but not so long ago a local doctor said he had come across the same practice in Borrowdale of all places – a sophisticated valley now, if ever there was one. Country children still pick and eat young hawthorn leaves, calling them 'bread and cheese', and an old Westmorland farmer says that there is nothing like young hawthorn leaves and elder shoots as a cure for boils. He, however, calls elder 'bull tree' and it is sometimes 'bour tree', too. It seems that, as a small boy, he was plagued with boils until his schoolmaster told him to gather elder and hawthorn on his way home, get his mother to seethe them and stand them all night, and drink the liquid next morning. It cured his boils and now, in old age, he is very lively, and he and his brother know a variety of simple cures – comfrey for bruises, figwort to draw 'spells' (thorns), and at this time of the year they make and eat herb pudding (as I do) but because it is delicious as well as 'cleansing'.

Lake District

There are many ways of telling whether a farm is a good and happy place and I have a private acid test – dogs, not the terrier by the door or the foxhound on summer vacation from the local pack but the working dogs. A sheepdog which lurks at the roadside ready to dash at traffic is a bad sign and so, too, is any matted, anxious dog, but a well-set-up one, who greets you readily, augurs well. Since 'good' and 'happy' farms are not necessarily synonymous one must differentiate – I know a shocking farm littered with broken machinery, muck up to the doors, where the dogs take a full and lively part with their master and, conversely, a good farm with a hard mistress whose temper is eased by consigning the dogs, howling, to the byre. Last week I went to a farm I have never visited before and was met by a dog smiling all over its face, nose almost touching tail in squirms of pleasure – and the test worked. This is the sort of farm one dreams of but seldom sees, now. The barn and byre doors had each a border of whitewash, the green picket fence was tipped with white and the cobbles swept clean and all this at the height of haying, done by one man and his wife. The dog led me past a barn-end where the shape and smoothness of the red sandstone block, leaning there, set me wondering. There is no such stone nearer than ten miles away, but there is a Roman fort on the hill above, and the Romans in this district seem to have had a liking for sandstone. Could it, I wonder, have started life as something else – perhaps even an altar stone – and been collected by some 'snapper-up of unconsidered trifles'. It certainly looks right where it is now.

Keswick

There is always a feeling of urgency by the end of July that one must catch the year in flight, for already some of the fields are cut for hay or silage and, though some are still bright with dog-daisies and field-geraniums, summer will not last for ever. Five kestrels were hatched over a month ago in the top of a tall pine tree and two fell, half-fledged, from the nest. One died quickly, the second lasted a few days and was taken, probably, by a fox, but three remain. These are almost ready for flight and I went to their wood, today, intending to watch them but found that road-machinery was, temporarily, based on the wood's edge. So I left hurriedly and wandered back over the fell along a forgotten footpath where the stone stiles in the walls are as perfect as they were scores of years ago, more like miniature stone staircases than mere stiles. Sun and cloud chased one another across the buttercup fields, the hedges are garlanded with wild roses, and the vale was full of colour. A pair of buzzards have a huge nest there and they rose, mewing, from it as I passed. The other side of the fell is much duller, the hayfields there are plain grass with few flowers, wire fences divide the fields, and some of the land, now empty of stock and the field-drains broken, has gone back to waste. It is a sad landscape and yet, on the edge of it is a field which, too, was over-grazed until lately. Today it was a thicket of orchids – of green tway-blade, pink-spotted orchids and the airy, green-white spikes of butterfly orchids. This is, indeed, swings and roundabouts, and no one need, it seems, despair of 'waste' land.

Keswick 5 June, 1972

Woods can be very deceptive. It is possible to walk through any wood and think that it is empty of animal life simply because animals have their own times and ways for living, with an added sense of what is right and usual and what is not. For instance, a forestry road is being driven up one of the fells – a disturbing and a clangorous business by any standard, especially when rock is being shifted – and yet the wild red-deer lie up, day-long, within hailing distance of all the upset. The men on the job see them often, couched in the undergrowth and seemingly inattentive, but let a walker or one man alone come and at once the deer are alert and, probably, away. I have often seen how deer will accept sheep and cattle and even humans who can stay still for long periods, and badgers are equally selective. The badgers who used to live in the now empty sett on the fell would come out at dusk and listen, heads veering like weather vanes, and – one could almost swear – counting the sounds. All the sounds from the farm below, clattering milk pails, dogs barking, men whistling and even a late tractor, were all passed over, but a rustle in the bracken got instant and wary attention.

Last night, I walked through another apparently deserted forest just after sunset with the last glow of light fingering through the dark spruces and a cold wind making a sound like surf in the trees. The ground was littered with new green shoots torn off by last week's gale. Nothing showed itself and yet the sense of being not alone, of being watched, was very strong indeed. It is comforting to look out across the miles of trees there and realise how safe a place this is and, personally, I am content not to see deer or badgers too easily; discretion is safer for them in this overcrowded land.

Keswick

Seldom, I think, has the identity of evening and morning
scent been more sharply cut than in this past week. The very
hot spell quietened everything during the middle hours of the
day, no birds stirred and the air was still, but at evening, with
an almost full, orange moon low on the fells, things came to
life. There was a movement in the air and the furious
scolding of a wren marked the passage of a hunting weasel
through the tangle of pinks, catmint and roses. Bats curved
up to the eaves and away in long sweeps down the hedges.
How different was the next morning. There had been rain in
the night and so it seemed a sensible time to go and look for
orchids in the Borrowdale bogs. The ground was very wet,
there were pools and runs of water in the bogs and each step
made a loud, sucking squelch. At first, the cold smell of
bog-water and moss predominated but, almost
imperceptibly, one became aware of other things. Many of
the spotted orchids and the small butterfly ones are almost
scentless, but bog asphodel and the fragrant orchids made up
for them with layers of sweetness. It was too early for the
dragonflies to be about but small, pale moths and black
chimney-sweepers were active and, again, it was a wren –
this time singing cheerfully in the crags above the bog – who
added what sound there was.

Keswick

Any day, any evening, is made up of ordinary, small things
but, given time and opportunity to look, these things are not
so very ordinary. Light has a lot to do with how you see
things, and this evening, with the declining sun shining into
the bottom of the narrow river-valley, everything looked
different and far from ordinary. The river ran quietly; moss-
capped stones and boulders broke its run so, in places, the
white water caught and threw back the glitter of sunlight.
The deeper, shaded pools shimmered with the green
reflections of rushes, alder and birch. Fish jumped.
Everything is very green now except where the sun lies
longest in the day and here betony, harebells and
honeysuckle compete in beauty and for space. The thickets of
wild raspberries, red with drooping fruit, are perhaps the

best places to be – and is it just by chance that the best of the thickets, one about a hundred yards long, is growing on ant-disturbed, ant-infested, rich earth? Much of this valley bottom is a sanctuary for ants because no plough has ever come here and it is to be hoped none ever will. The ant-hills – some busy, some seemingly quiet – are often grassed over and sprigged with thyme or heather and some must be very old. The broken edge of one hill in the raspberry canes showed not only its small orange-yellow working ants but some winged ones and several large winged females, presumably ready for mating flights. There were discarded wings on some of the hummocks so it seems that some mating is over. No ants were flying so late in the day but the low sun caught clouds of other flying insects and turned them to gold. A green woodpecker was hanging about – they are often in this part of the valley, understandably, for ant-hills provide them with quite a part of their rations in winter. Winter seemed far ahead, however, this evening.

Keswick 4 June, 1973

There are times – few and far between, most often early or late in the day – when some trick of light or weather turns back time and restores to the countryside a long-lost quietness and a look it had many years ago. It was so yesterday evening. The meadows on the ridge, where the Castle Rigg stone circle stands, were washed by late sunlight, yellow with buttercups and lively with bird-song. Linnets sang from a flowering ash, skylarks rose singing too, and a peewit called along the lane, but the far valley was softened by mist – no dwelling, no road was there to see. The ridge was a world apart. Oddly enough, one can occasionally catch the same feeling of time turned back even near a busy farm. There is a huddle of farm buildings not far away, solid farm houses, cottages, barns and byres of what was once a hard-working hamlet, now partially in decay. Cows are stalled in part of an immense barn, bigger and higher than many country churches, but they do not take it all. One end is given over to hay and tackle; a calf, penned in a corner, blares quietly to itself, but if you go outside and up a flight of stone steps you find a gallery under the roof where cobwebs, clotted with dust and age, barely move in the air. There are two very big oak chests there; one has one long lid, the other has four – pale and smooth with age – and all stand open, letting out the warmth and sweetness of cattle foods. Indeed, you could imagine there was still the sweetness of malt on the air. That is, I think, hindsight, knowing that there was once the malthouse of a brewery on this site. There is a stone ball on the roof corner outside which is said to be the sign of a brewery. Is this true, I wonder?

Keswick

23 July, 1973

It is seldom that anyone who lives in the country and gardens, or keeps bees, or picks and preserves their own fruit gets any leisure at this time of the year to stand and stare – to take time, even in the longest day, to be plainly idle. The summer days here are usually over-full and yet, today, for reasons quite beyond my control, there was almost a whole day to watch the hours go by and to see what they had in them. I have, sadly, no hive bees now but there was time to watch other people's bees busy on the white clover on the lawn and on the more ordinary garden flowers (modern roses have no nectar worth speaking about and little pollen). The bumble-bees who work so much harder had been out since early light and, in the noonday hours, they were joined by hoverflies and a wandering dragonfly who darted and hovered in the hot sun. There was time, too, to watch the wren feeding her now noisy young in their nest in the dark corner above the side door – she is fearless, singing with loud confidence, and seeing far more of me than I of her. The late afternoon, too, was leisurely and there was time to lean on a gate (a country-dweller's traditional but seldom-used prerogative) and let the smells and sounds of summer soak into a quiet mind. A lonely strip of meadow, deep in grass and flowers, part marsh and willow-edged, stretches from the gate to a far wood and there was just enough air stirring to bow the grasses but not the willows and to spread the unforgettable scents of ripening grass and burgeoning meadowsweet and – alien and yet not – the tang of a distant sheep dip.

Keswick

The quietening hand of the sun, of heat, lies across the valley and the fells now from mid-morning to the late hours of the day and, apart from the heat, time and sheep wait for no one – so I was out early one morning lately armed with a square of wire netting and some sticks. My goal was a dry and stony fellside where, last June, the sheep ate the only flowering spikes of the small white orchid (*Leucorchis albida*) near here. It is 'local in hill pastures – rare elsewhere' – certainly not food for sheep. I met the sheep and their lambs as I slid down the steep path: they surged up from a thicket of thorn, closely followed by the shepherd and his dog. The dog was lolloptongued and panting and, by now, all three of us were wet with dew and sweat, for it was a close and sticky morning, grey from fell to fell, with thunderheads piled high above Helvellyn's ridge. I netted the orchids and found two new plants as the first drops of rain fell and a cuckoo – tune still unchanged – went calling up the valley. The evening was very different, by then the air and the sky were clear, so the sinking sun left behind it a glow of copper-gilt, the mountains sharp-cut, and a blue haze across the valley. I waited in a deserted garden at the edge of a high wood to see what came and, as I waited, the whole hill seemed to stir, to breathe and to come alive. There were rustlings in the underbrush, robins sang so softly as to be almost inaudible, and then – with shattering suddenness, a roebuck barked – right beside me but hidden by the green. It was angry at an invasion of its demesne and assertive of its rights, as well it should be – this is its place, not mine.

Keswick

There has been some good rain lately and today, sandwiched in between a wet morning and a wetter evening, there was a hot and sunny afternoon which gave a sparkle to the fells more akin to spring than to July. There was a liveliness in the air which has been missing of late and it was very evident in a series of bogs, rising one above another, in pockets of land on a steep fellside. These are small bogs and everything in them seems small too. Most of their flowers are 'common' – and none the worse for that – bog asphodel is just opening its sweet-smelling spikes and spotted and fragrant orchids stand beside them only overtopped by the silvery fluff of cotton-grass. Pink cross-leaved heath (visited today by sooty chimney-sweeper moths) winds amongst the bog mosses and dips into the now noisy becks which edge the wet places. It is below orchid-level, however, that the best things are – the small white flowers of flycatching sundew, vivid blue milkwort and the soft pink trumpets of bog pimpernel, which is so much more like a minute convolvulous than a pimpernel. The dry, brackeny slopes between the bogs were hot. A lizard rustled off at my feet and grasshoppers – every hue of green and yellow – sailed off ahead and a young hen pheasant (perhaps too well fed on grasshoppers) was almost too lazy to shift. The only growth of any size in the bogs is the ancient junipers – maybe two hundred years old – whose green awl-like leaves make as they fall (unlike those of other cypresses) an excellent bed for small plants. Today a party of new-on-the-wing blue tits, only greeny-yellow as yet, were using a juniper as a staging post – they were noisy, pancake-landers as cheerful as the sunny afternoon.

Keswick

Flags – what does the word conjure up for you? Is it proud emblems snapping in the wind, a bird's quill feather, the sweet flags of the fens (once used for strewing), or the stone-flags of kitchen floors? Here, in Cumbria, flags are the yellow irises which sometimes take over whole marshy fields, edge rivers and clothe marshes. They are not sweet at all and stock avoid them, but on the lake levels they give cover to nesting snipe and yellow wagtails. The young wagtails are on the wing now but are greeny-yellow, not shining like their parents or the yellow flags.

Just as a word may have many meanings so a known place like the lake-marshes can present a different face, offer different things, even on consecutive days. Ten days ago the lake was already low and there was little flow in the river. The only stir was from clouds of diminutive fishes in the shallows and there was something else – a long, pale fish lying quite still in deep water. It was over two feet long, mottled olive-grey above and pale beneath, snake-like. It was a dead sea-lamprey whose open, round sucker-mouth with its double teeth and toothed tongue looked, if possible, even more vicious dead than alive. It must have travelled almost a score of miles from the Solway through Workington town and Cockermouth, up the Derwent, and the length of Bassenthwaite Lake to spawn here in fresh water – and to die. I went back very early this morning but there were no other lampreys and the flags are almost over, but the fresh yellow waterlilies stand up, glittering, above an even wider sea of mud.

Keswick   28 July, 1975

'It is fitting in European Heritage Year (says a leading cement company) to be reminded of the scale of plant used to provide the raw materials for buildings which make up our heritage,' and to mark this they have restored a classic lime kiln at East Lothian. What of other kilns in Britain? Lime burning for mortar (and, later, for lime for acid land) is very old. Indeed, the Romans made so durable a lime mortar that it outlasted some of the stones it held. Cumbria is rich in kilns from Morecambe Bay to the Border and their diversity in age, structure, and siting is equally rich – method is all they have in common, that varies little. Limestone was layered with wood, peat, or charcoal (and later, coal or coke) and fired to make calcium oxide and quick lime. I have favourites. Some are on the Kendal limestone – one in the Lyth Valley is sunk in a green tree-shade and has a double hearth, another on treeless Orton Scar is stark and open. One, over thirty miles to the north-west, stands alone facing the ancient British fort on Carrock Fell and there is an almost secret group near the ruined house above Ireby which Hugh Walpole took for the 'Fortress' in his Herries novels. One of these has four hearths and is smothered in a tangle of nettles and briars. None, however, can beat for siting the kiln which stands on the Roman Wall at Pike Hill above Lanercost. It is over twenty feet tall and has a splendid 'Gothic' arch. The chimney down which the stone was tipped is overgrown with bushes now, and is choked with cool, green hart's-tongue fern, but even the wall and its turret alongside look small by comparison. Surely it, too, could be a candidate for heritage?

Keswick 25 August, 1975

Many fell farms, nowadays, suffer from a lack of labour – at one time with more loosely knit families there always seemed to be an old uncle about, an active grandfather and a boy or two to tackle odd jobs. Gates and walls got mended, footpaths seen to and there was help for the hay and the harvest; even the nettles and thistles got cut before they set seed. Those days are gone in the main, and today I talked with two farmers with differing views on thistles. One, with a busy milkround and little help, advocated spraying; the other with sons and a more leisurely way said you must keep at them – cut early and knock down the stragglers. Be that as it may, there is a wealth of seeding thistles on a wilder land and the moorland round the tarn is silvered, now, with thistledown. This is fundamentally fair land – short turf jewelled with the many-coloured faces of heartsease. But spear, marsh and scotch thistles are all spreading havoc. There is even thistledown on the tarn, caught in the pale flowers of water lobelia and the fluffy heads of the bur-reed. It is on the backs of the grazing sheep and it drifts down lazily to the valley fields. Only the goldfinches profit. But the thistles do not have their own way everywhere. It was very quiet at the farm in mid-afternoon, no dog barked and there was not the usual clatter of voices, only one sister busy at the slop-stone. Where was the other? She was out 'scopping t'trash', taking a sickle to the nettles and the thistles. There seems to be no use for thistles, but nettles are different, food plants for butterflies, eatable in spring, once used for coarse cloth and for nettle beer. I have an old recipe book which speaks of nettle beer which 'may be seen advertised in humble shops in Manchester and elsewhere'. But not any more, I think.

Keswick

It was only nine o'clock when the badger first poked its black and white mask up from the sett mouth – a very early appearance for this time of the year but a wet dusk had come early after a day of soft, continuous rain which still pattered on the leaves overhead confusing sound and heightening the scents of June – wet grass, elderflowers and honeysuckle. There has been no occupant of this sett for some time. It is at the top of a shaly bank made, now, to look steeper than it is by the spires of flowering foxgloves. The badger, at each testing sniff, seemed to sense rather than see that the accustomed pattern of the hawthorn twenty yards below was somehow awry, somehow wrong, so it took its time. When it did come – a last year's cub, very loose-limbed and nimble with a white-bobbed, bushy tail – it was quite at ease. It crossed the sett, leisurely, pausing there, too, to sniff and disappeared into the brambly wood. A wren and a willow warbler plotted its progress with only ritual scoldings and later its pawmarks were plain in the mud down the lane.

The red campions had lost their colour in the dusk and the sky was emptied of late-flying swallows when, again, there was a slight stir in the trees and a young one-pronged roebuck stepped delicately down. It, too, distrusted the hawthorn pattern and craned its neck, even turning three complete circles – perhaps hoping that the jigsaw would have settled, but its nose warned and it, too, turned back to the wood and I, wet and midge-bitten, turned for home. But what more could anyone ask of a June night?

Keswick

The recent hot nights have been good for badger-watching. Badgers – like humans – long for the comparative cool of evening and are impatient to be above ground. Indeed, I know more about who and what lives where than for two years. The glow of sunset is slow to fade and the mountains look as if cut from blue-grey card, sharp at the edges. The smell of honeysuckle is sweet, drowned sometimes by new hay, but along the beck in the high valley there is an indefinable scent – wild roses, perhaps, and water mint, but the dark flow of water is both a frontier to the badgers' territory and a barrier to scent. It carries its own flow of cool air. I waited, one evening lately, on the opposite bank and the hay machines had only just stopped when first one small black and white head and then a second emerged on to the narrow ledge near the top of the fern-clad bluff. These are this year's cubs and, careless with never a sniff or a look, they set off up the narrow badger track. The first cub was yards ahead when, with no warning and a thump, a wood pigeon landed on the fence above their heads. Panic reigned. The leader turned, scrabbling frantically, only to collide head-on with the second who was also trying to turn – small stones shot down into the beck, ferns wobbled wildly, and there was a general tangle of grey, white and green. The pigeon left in alarm, but out of the muddle they came and over the skyline at a fast run and I did not see them again, clearly, but later two small shapes were rummaging along the hay rows in search of beetles and slugs. My homeward lanes were pale with wild roses in the dusk and soft with the flight of moths.

Keswick   *10 August, 1976*

It seems astonishing that so distinctive a tree as a mulberry can get overlooked – but some do. The mulberries of Cumbria occupy varied places, fruiting well at Holker Hall near Grange-over-Sands and in the garden of the Cheshire Home at Windermere. These are youngish trees but some in a vicarage garden near Duddon are said to have been planted by Huguenot refugees to feed their silk worms, and leaves from a very old tree at Keswick went to feed silk worms in Kent during the last war. But there is one mulberry tree which, to me, is a tree on its own in every sense. It stands quite alone, below a limestone ridge facing north to the Carlisle plain in what looks like an ordinary empty field. Close scrutiny, however, reveals a well-paved road in the grass, a sunken square where the tree stands, a pillar in a field wall and remains of fallen walls – some in the tree itself. It is reputed to be about three hundred years old but is still a noble tree, some limbs still standing tall, some fallen and already rooted. Its heart-shaped leaves shine in the sun and its fruit is just turning colour. Legend says that when there was warning of a Scots raid, the dwellers in the now lost house used to hide in the tree – taking their pigeons with them and,

as the raiders got near, they released the birds who flew out
giving an impression of pigeons disturbed in an empty tree.
But what, I wonder, happened in winter?

Keswick   5 September, 1977

The lately controversial bridge which carries the A66 over
the gorge of the river Greta, east of Keswick, is not
noticeable if you drive across it. It is better to walk over for it
gives a clear view of the western fells. Better still, try
walking under it. The bridge has its own stark beauty, seen
from below, with its rather flat, springing arches carried on
tall slightly fluted columns which play games with light and
shade. It is new-looking at present but time, of course, will
alter that just as it has altered this narrow valley. It is quiet
now but once it must have been a bustling place and while
one must salute the men who built the bridge one should
never forget the men who, about 1567, drove the still-
existent tunnel through the solid rock beyond and almost
below the bridge on the south side of the river. It was done
the hard way to carry the water for the furnace bellows and
stamp-houses at Brigham where the ore (mined in Newlands
beyond Derwentwater and ferried across the lake) was
smelted. The industry went on until the Civil War when it
was destroyed but even then the water was used at The Forge
for a variety of small mills, forges, and works until a few
years ago. All the sounds were soothing, down by the river,
this evening – the rush of water over the rocks, the near-
constant sound of traffic overhead, and the whistle and splash
of a pair of mallard settling for the night in a backwater. The
water is gathered to the tunnel by a long curved weir whose
timber top is still securely bolted to its stone base even
though runs of water fall through it over curtains of green
moss to nourish a wealth of rosebay willow herb, orange and
yellow mimulus, and tall reeds. The sluice for the tunnel is
permanently closed now but water gets through – deep and
dark it lies almost up to the tunnel roof – and I wished as I
walked along the green path alongside its hidden length that
it could be drained – just once – to see what it is really like
inside and how the old men who made it and who still seem
to haunt the place had gone about their work so long ago.

Keswick

10 July, 1978

Old meadows and isolated fields on marginal fell land here
can often tell much of their past history if you look hard
enough: although farms and barns can fall into decay and
field walls subside into stone-based green lines, the plants,
given luck, stay. They often also have an oral tradition. I
think especially of one high field. It is a place of contrasts
with a green ghyll running up into the mountainside, down
which a bitter air can come, holding the ash leaves back until
June and the hawthorn blossom until Midsummer Day, but
one side of it is thick with primroses in spring and its south-
facing slope is now a wealth of flowers. Most of them are
common things but there are fragrant orchids too, a few
butterfly orchids, and even an odd northern marsh orchid.
Small heath butterflies and little black chimney-sweep moths
hesitate over them and the shorter turf is a sea of mountain
pansies in every change of purple and yellow. Why is this
field here and why is it as it is? An ancient fell-enclosure wall
defines one side and a conifer wood another, and the open fell
above sweeps up to over a thousand feet. Tradition has it that
this was once a small prized hayfield for a farm down the
ghyll and in a fine July the whole family would come up with
scythes, wooden hayrakes, and market baskets of food and
drink for the haymaking. But that was long ago and now the
field is lightly stocked with Exmoor ponies (surely, pre-Ice
Age, some of the older dwellers in Britain?) and though they
may tread on some orchids or roll on a few pansies they are
easy on the land and dung it well. Indeed, the sour and rushy
fields below the wall are in sharp contrast and make one
wonder what the future could hold for these flowering acres
if their present owner – mindful alike of her land and of her
ponies – was no longer here. Too many fields face the same
sort of threat here and elsewhere.

Keswick

24 July, 1978

A lifetime in the Lake District and over a quarter of a century
of writing Country Diaries are making me wonder if it is
time to seek danger money – but from and for what? Most
hazards are small if you respect the fells and watch your feet
and the weather. There are sheep ticks if badger-watching in

bracken, and deer ticks in scrub and once a usually quiet work-horse, having trodden in a wasp's nest, thundered down a steep fell and over a watched sett with all the impetus and abandon of a tank out of control.

Once a roebuck – generally self-effacing – turned nasty, menacing me with its head down, leading tines pointed forward, but then I had come on a 'roe-ring' in a thicket in July. One October dusk a red stag, with its hinds at its back, and a younger stag down the wood, looked quite willing to add me to the snags for removal, roaring angrily and tossing clods in the air.

Now the menace looks very ordinary – cows. This summer I have been watching a pair of fox cubs where, two years ago, young cows shared the field and were quite content with the odd snort down my neck or a lick up the ear as I sat, stone-still waiting, but now things are different. The cows are grown into massive black and white beasts and, currently, much given to rough cow-play. At first they just went in for a bit of barging and head-clashing amongst themselves but one full moon night lately (are cows affected by the moon?) they included me in their games, ending up with a kicking-up of back legs.

I left. Last night I could not – dare not – go near the earth. Am I getting soft? Victorian? I think not – a farmer I know, no small or timid man, says that in a like predicament he 'ran like hell'.

Keswick   7 August, 1978

Late summer is not a good time here: the air is often humid and thundery, inducing laziness which is no good with a heavy crop of raspberries to pick and weeds to keep at bay, so a damp morning is a good excuse to get up out of the valley even for a few hours, a thousand feet or so. The fell sheep and their lambs were down from the tops and confined to the yards for a late clipping and general overlooking as I passed the farm early in the day. The noise was considerable – high, plaintive baas and deeper reassurances from the separated ewes and lambs; but the dogs, their job temporarily done, were silent and the swifts, hawking round the barns, were silent, too. There were clouds of flies (missing the sheep?) all the way up the ghyll but they fell away as the higher air thinned and lightened, leaving the moortop to rush moths, meadow pipits and the ever-present crows. A solitary sheep who must have evaded the round-up fed peacefully on what, in normal years, is a treacherous blanket bog but now is just a green rush-and-sphagnum mound. But the recent rain has at least made the beck up there run clear and clean again. A heron, up from the valley too, veered off from my place on a springy bank of pink-flowered, cross-leaved heath at the beck's edge and, as time passed, several very small trout and one big enough to leave a bow wave went down the pool. A young frog took off and dived into the water with barely a ripple. I am, it seems, safer than herons. It is going to be a good year for blaeberries: already some are big and dark and ready, as Culpeper says, 'to give a purplish colour to hands and lips that handle them'. He considered that it was a pity that they were not more used in physic for hot agues and to cool the liver, but I am content to eat them as I sit and forget the raspberries and the weeds.

Keswick   *1 September, 1979*

Many of the best things are come-by-chance – like the two tall self-sown birches in this garden. They are more than forty years old now and invaluable for what they attract as well as interesting in the comments they evoke from some visitors to the house. Most people look straight between them and across the valley and the lake to the fells beyond, but some notice them as trees. Two men, both now dead, had had very different views. One, a doctor, said very confidentially: 'I'd have that (the birch nearer the house) down if it were mine; it spoils the view.' But the other, who was once a working forester and later the president of the Royal Forestry Society, called it 'a lovely tree' on several occasions and hoped it would never be taken down – and I hope so, too. This morning the thin pattern of its lowest branches is outlined against the bright green fields of autumn fog and the first flush of heather on the slopes of Scawdel Fell across Derwentwater. The birches are staging posts now for southward-moving birds, mostly warblers – yellow-green wood warblers and more sober-coloured willow and chiffchaff warblers. Only the willow warblers nested near here, the others have been scarce this sad, wet year. A sparrowhawk makes unexpected sweeps through the garden but, so far, has got no warblers; they stay well within the trees. But the greenfinches – slower and more apt to sit on the tops of things – are less lucky and some of their greeny feathers lie under the hawk's feathering posts. But it is not just birds who come – there is the occasional red squirrel, the bats who hunt round them in the dusk and hedgehogs who forage in the roots after dark. There are come-by-chance plants, too: mullein, brown fox-tail fennel, borage and wild angelica. The tall mullein is a yellow and grey accent in the shorter growth, the fennel is useful in the kitchen; the borage, as Gerard says, makes the heart glad, and the angelica brings cheerful crowds of hoverflies on sunny days. But the autumn crocuses and the cyclamen will flourish best in the light shade of the birches. It all is very remote from the busy holiday town and valley below.

Keswick   *17 September, 1979*

The solid sandstone farm and outbuildings at Banks Foot, east and a little above Lanercost Priory, an Augustinian foundation like Carlisle and Hexham, look down on the Irthing Valley. They are a trap for the sun and the afternoon warmth, which today were held there in the maze of walls and barns and especially so in the little garth to one side of the house. It was an orchard once and old lichened apple trees stand in the angle of two of its walls which have built into them four bee boles – long out of use but still in good shape. Boles – recesses – made to shelter straw bee-skeps before there were wooden hives, often face south and east, but these are unusually shallow, only twelve inches into the stone – but they have wide stone sills jutting further out. Their height and depth varies between two and three feet. It was very quiet and peaceful in the garth. The grass had been cut recently and there was the sweet smell of its drying as well as the sharp scent of green elder shoots where they had been pushed back from the boles, and both mixed with the air from the oak trees and the tang of muck from the yard over the wall. Three of the boles held tangles of rusty iron – hasps, hinges and curlicues from an old gate – but the fourth had the discarded home of a mouse, a small silky sausage of dry grass and fine stems. I did not disturb it, but when I went round into the yard it was obvious where its materials (and its owner?) had come from. The bee bole wall is lined with four low stalls, roofed with slate, and out of use now but thick inside with soft cobwebs and old hay. There is another wall beyond them and then a ruinous horse gin, its six-sectioned slate roof sagging on an intricate beam pattern and its machinery all gone. It will not last much longer – not like the Roman Wall (a turf wall at this western end) which crossed Banks Burn above the farm.

Keswick
23 June, 1980

A weaving pattern of bats has been flying here against a clear, sunset sky. I wish I knew more about their ways, but a nationwide bat survey is going on – so there is hope. There have been bats over this garden for at least thirty years in fairly consistent numbers (except, perhaps, after hard winters) but, sadly, none in my roof. They used to come and go from the gabled end of the next house and then, for no obvious reason, moved to another house. One of their first landlords disliked them and called the pest officer, who firmly said they were a protected species, but the second one accepts them happily – after all, he once walked ankle-deep and shoeless in dried bat dung in a deserted Indian mosque, and did not find that objectionable. We usually see them first in April or early May, hunting zealously even on cold nights, and then they disappear for at least a month. This April there were pipistrelles as usual and one much larger which kept apart – was it a daubenton's bat? Now, as last June, there are between eight and a dozen; are these new families? A city cat spent last summer here and he and the bats seemed to have a mutual fascination. He was a dark tabby, but when he sat on the lawn in the dusk the bats swooped down and round his head so that he flicked it up to show his shining white bib. Did it attract them as pale moths do? My sister and I, as little girls, were told that bats came to white things, so we waited in the dusk in white pinafores and self-induced shivers, for it was also said that if a bat tangled in your hair, you became blind. They nearly touched our heads, but never quite. There seem to have been fewer moths these last years but last night, in a damp and misty half-dark, the air under the trees was alive with their soft flight – good for the bats – and good to see so many again.

Keswick

The early hours of the day are the best ones even in a cool summer like this. There is a quality, then, in the light before sun-up which throws things into sharp relief which full daylight overwhelms – the silver of the wet grass in the valley and the beaded silver of a perfect spider's web across my door. But the sun soon gets warm on the bony ridge where the Castle Rigg stone circle stands looking two ways – over the lakes to the western fells and eastwards to the Pennine hills. On 1 July, this year, looking from that ridge, there was not a cut hayfield to be seen but there was every other green from fell bracken and blaeberry to the sheen of soon-to-be-cut meadows. Indeed, at the farm on the next rise the lads were just leaving the cobbled yard with the tractors early in the day to start hay-timing for 1980. 'Hay-timing' is an expression you seldom hear used now, but for an older generation it still calls up recollections of whole families helping in the hayfields and of covered baskets and bottles (mainly of cold tea) being taken out for ten o'clock. There are still some fields uncut, now red with sorrel or white with dog-daisies – but some of the first-shorn fields are already greening and cows are out on them to get what they can and manure the fog. Only marginal land nowadays can flaunt the pink ragged-robin, blue field-geranium and the tall meadowsweet. This looks a timeless land – and so it is – but there are pegs on which time can be hung. There is the circle, the farm buildings and the names of the fields and the 'lost' Roman road which came to Keswick from the east at Voreda, Old Penrith, and whose course is yet uncertain.

Keswick

Today the afternoon hours were quiet and heavy; nothing stirred on the stony fellside above the narrow valley where the river Greta and the disused railway line cross and recross one another many times. This slope was, until a few years ago, more or less inaccessible, a thicket of thorns and crab-apple trees with hidden clearings and a place where the small white orchid grew. But the land was needed for stock, improved, so the thickets and the flowers went (but the thorns are springing stubbornly from buried roots) and road waste was strewn along it. So the grass is sparse yet and the shorn ewes, looking bony and sharp-angled until their new wool springs, dozed benignly in the warmth while their fat lambs – past playing – fed alone. The long upsweep of Lonscale Fell and Saddleback across the valley, with the cone of Calva between, reared up in sunlight but with thunderheads to the far north. Strangely, the air was lighter and livelier in the valley bottom, perhaps because of the rush of the river and the coolness it carries with it. The growth on the old line was luxuriant for a few years after the last train went but then the fences sagged and the animals got in. Now, though, there are still primroses in spring and harebells in August, the green of bramble, wild raspberry and broom are hard-chewed. I sat on the high river-bank looking down into the brown water, thinking of the plod back and envying a buzzard who floated over to settle in an oak whorl gently below it; a summer-red roe-deer came out to graze on a small green lawn in the fern. The flies were tormenting – it twitched its rump, flicked its tail, and its dark velvet ears were in constant movement. Time stopped, but when it went I went too, but with opened eyes. I saw fresh roses on the berried briars, a second flowering on the crabs and, at my feet, a flock of purple mountain pansies.

Keswick   *15 September, 1980*

There are still swallows skimming round the green mossed roofs of the barn at the foot of the fell, and still fresh meadowsweet in the wet places by the beck. The rowanberries hang, deeply red, but the sloes are green – barely touched with purple – and a wren, singing loudly, is hidden by green-fruited brambles. The easterly air, some hundreds of feet up, has a cool touch indeed; this is a season unlike any other for some years – the rainy summer saw to that. But why is there such a prodigal wealth of flowers on the grass-of-Parnassus; is the rain the cause of that, too? It is flowering in one place on the fell where there has been none for ten years and, in another which usually has a few spikes, it is everywhere. Standard floras say that *Parnassia palustris* is 'widespread but local' – a way of saying, to me, that you are lucky to find it. It grows strongly in the wet dune slacks of south Cumbria but here, in the high fells, it is more ethereal and yet more at home. The white, five-petalled flowers are heavily veined, faintly scented, and their five cream stamens alternate with delicate green-fingered scales. This morning the whole fell-top was unusual – not its sober self. A cloud of swallows went over low at a thousand feet, a flock of meadow pipits bounced in and out of the fading heather; and, unexpectedly, a grouse called. This is not a grouse moor as it once was. The heather, latterly, has become overgrown, but some was burned systematically in spring and there is new growth. Will there be new grouse in residence in spring? I turned to come home; it was only 9 a.m. but already the sun was misting over, and minute by minute the far blue of the Scottish hills faded into nothingness.

Keswick   25 May, 1981

It is about a hundred years since the brewers left their building in this stream-loud ghyll for a bigger place in the neighbouring market town, so it is surely imagination that the smell of grain, of malt, still hangs in the gloom of the ancient walls and the worm-eaten beams, and rises from the damp cobbles of the floor. All is silent and shuttered, the tall arched doors – big enough to take horses and carts – are chained, and chains and hooks hang unused on the inner walls. The horse-stalls are empty and the maze of echoing rooms is thick with cobwebs and clotted with dust and fallen plaster. A narrow, near-vertical wooden stair with a rope rail leads to the upper floor – do not trust the boards – and here the dust and plaster are even thicker, especially in the rusted iron grate. Swallows have found their way in down a shaft of sunlight. The rush and clamour of water is loud everywhere within and without. One outside wall overhangs the stream precariously, and below it huge slabs of slate jut out; some lie in the flow and others on the opposite bank from a long-tumbled bridge. Steps go down to what was once the cottagers' only water supply, and here a pair of dippers, whose nest is in a dry culvert, bob on the stones, protesting at intrusion. A slight air – water-borne – ruffles the new leaves on the ashes; ivy-leafed speedwell and bluebells hug the bank. Greater celandine and blue-flowered green alkanet crowd the wall corners – a perfect May morning? It only lacks a cuckoo.

Keswick

A steady breeze blew down the stream-divided valley this afternoon and two cuckoos calling from either slope made their own antiphon, sometimes louder, sometimes softer. The whole valley and the sky seemed to be in motion, for though the high clouds went leisurely in the blue sky the haygrass was bent to silver as the wind went over and the young sycamore leaves were bent sideways. It even bent the stiff flag leaves below a foxes' earth (once a badger's sett) on the other bank where three fox cubs played, rolled and pounced in the sun. They often paused to listen and to look, evidently expecting a parent with food. They are well past the baby stage – all legs, ears and darkening coats – soon they will be on their own and what will lie ahead? Will it be a discreet life on the fell, a shorter one around some farm, or death on the road or with the hunt in autumn? This golden afternoon and the months until, say, September, are easy for little foxes. I left them to their play and walked higher up the flooded, peat-brown water to settle in a warm hollow. There is a deep pool in that place under green ferns and arching wild roses where a water shrew lives. Today it was swimming in search of food; its small head and bright eyes just clear of the water, ready to leap at any mayfly which floated too near the surface. Sometimes, too, it dived in a bubble of silver air held by its fur and sometimes it was hidden in the fern for minutes. It, too, has a family to feed but at least they should be safe from anything except, perhaps, a now too-invasive mink.

Keswick

This could be called the history of a field, perhaps of many fields now, but this one is on a valley slope edged with trees on three sides. Fifty years ago it had a lodge in one corner and a well-kept drive to a fine house. It was grazed only periodically. The turf had moonwort and adder's tongues in spring; in summer there were orchids – tway-blade, fragrant and butterfly ones – and, in autumn, betony and scabious, all good for moths and butterflies. There were mushrooms, too. Then the estate was broken up and the timber was felled in a wood at the field's edge and dragged out smashing many field-drains so that springs broke out in the grass. Gorse and briars grew on the drive but still tree pipits sang and nested at its top. In latter years, however, it had too many sheep and horses with foals and the ground grew poorer but the ultimate disaster was ponies. They churned up the wet ground with their hooves, chewed the hedges and tore up even the coarsest grass in winter. Then they were given hay balls which fetched sorrel and docks. But in spring they were banished. Today I was asked back after the land had been fed and – suddenly – time was turned back to my childhood days. The adder's tongue and the moonwort have gone, maybe for ever, but there are orchids – tway-blade, a few spotted orchids and armies of butterfly ones, greeny-white and sweet to smell. Dusky chimney-sweeper moths wavered over the tall grasses and a fat orange underwing was deep in its roots. I am told that there may, soon, be cows but perhaps some of the flowers will stay?

Keswick   3 August, 1981

Brown flood water rushed under Walk Mill bridge today where usually in July there is only a gentle flow. There had been a near-cloudburst above on the fell overnight and even the grassy oblong of land above the bridge was water-logged. If I was a betting woman I would lay that it was once the pond for the walk mill – a mill for fulling cloth. It is called 'the garden' locally and though there is no sign left of the mill except the name, there are some fields higher up which are called 'tenters', a sure indication of use for stretching and drying cloth. Sometimes, in these water-gifted valleys, it is only the names which remain of the old mills which made cotton or woollen cloth, bobbins and thread, gunpowder and lead pencils. They also supplied power for forges, for sawing, grinding corn and even for threshing. It has been far too wet lately to explore the stream-sides overgrown with grass, meadowsweet and barbed wild roses and today it seemed better to get in from the weather to the shelter of a long-disused mill. Some of its machinery is still there as well as two mill stones but it was the small, overlooked and cobwebbed things which brought the past very near. A child's hoop hung on a wall and a pair of clog irons leant on a sill. There was an ancient wooden hayrake and a rusted gripe (a strong fork for digging) in a corner and dead leaves everywhere. Cold air sifted in through gaps in the slates and hanging trails of ivy swung gently in the green silence.

The Border
31 August, 1981

The air on this high Border land, stranded between England and Scotland, seems clearer and sweeter than anywhere else at the onset of autumn. It is an empty land, and puzzling until you remember its comparatively recent past when men from both sides went raiding and reiving; later its straight tracks and small roads were drove-ways for the black Scottish cattle. They came south in autumn to fatten for the spring fairs, which began in Cumberland in April. The typically wide verges now are bright with harebells and heather. Green rushes are being harvested for winter bedding. Sometimes patterned cultivation runs up a cleft into the hills; sometimes spruce blankets the poorer slopes. Many of the grey stone buildings have still an embattled look; but some are long and low, once used for animals at one end and people at the other. But in one group of farm buildings round a house dated 1765, there is one small round 'house' which seems to defy identification. It is solid stone and perfectly round, about twenty feet high and about the same in diameter. Its walls are whitewashed and, halfway up, its conical stone slate roof tapers to a single crowning stone. It is not a dovecote although the shape suggests it, nor – I think – a corn-drying kiln. A stone runnel comes out from its only door and its two windows are a later addition. It must have been too small, too airless, for a pound for beasts. Was it a pound for felons? There was, once, no lack of those and tradition has it that a magistrate lived 'up the road'.

Keswick
24 May, 1982

May mornings and the voices of cuckoos are inextricably mixed in the minds of many country people. But it was afternoon when the cuckoos were calling across the raised bog on the Solway coast. The tide was full in the Firth and hundreds of oystercatchers, a solid mass of black and white, waited patiently for their turn on the last shingle bar before the saltings, now white with flowering scurvy grass. Pairs of shelducks waited, too, while curlews and dunlin idled along the sea turf where the nets of the fishermen were drying. A lot of gorse was killed in January and the early May gale caught the first green on the beeches lining the road so that, seen from a distance, they are a mosaic of newer green and seared, coppery-brown – very strange against a thundery sky in sunlight. A cuckoo, silent now, skimmed past to drop into the bents and into a furious attack from a pair of meadow pipits. They seemed to know its intent all too well and dashed with astonishingly vicious force. They drove it away several times but it always came back to the same spot and other pipits joined in. They flew in its face and one little one even jumped, clawing, on its back, making it throw up its head, open a surprisingly scarlet gape and hiss. The home-coming school bus trundled ponderously down the road and stopped – too much for a cuckoo, but they do not give up easily.

Keswick   *6 June, 1982*

There are still small parcels of land – triangles of acid meadow, small stretches of limestone, quarries and coppices – on the edge of the Lake District which are left to their own devices, immune from 'improvement' or interference. One such meadow is beside a stream in a valley, sheltered by mountains from the north and with fells to the south low enough to let in the day-long sun. Winter, it is said, stays here until June, but now summer has come. The hay is getting tall but in this overlooked triangle the rust-red flowers of water-avens out-top the varied grasses. Purple wood-geraniums and yellow-gold globe flowers edge the water, catching and holding the sunlight. The ashes are still leafless, and there is a badger track below them, obvious to an interested eye. Another piece of land, to the north of Skiddaw, is tilted to a long view of the Scottish hills and the towers of Chapel Cross. It is on a road which goes nowhere, serves no farm, and only joins two other quiet roads. It was a very small quarry, once, and now its limestone slabs lie buried in deep grass and nettles. There are rings of cowslips and early purple orchids; soon there will be frog orchids. Already there are budded thickets of *Genista tinctoria*, dyers' greenweed, on the tops of the narrow ridges, catching every air from the sea. This plant is the source, with woad, of the famous green which labelled Falstaff's 'misbegotten knaves in Kendal Green'. What have they in common, these two places? Nothing, except that no one wants them save the wagtails by the beck and the larks on the hill.

Keswick   *3 July, 1983*

It seems foolish these nights to waste time by coming home to bed – so many lost and unreturning hours while the summer half-light and the moonlight, together, fade towards dawn. The day's heat often draws moisture from the land and, after sunset, it lies along the high, narrow valley and its beck, softening every contour and filling every hollow. The white May blossom on the isolated fellside thorns floats like snow above the mist and the muted green of the fields. There were, last night, few sounds by the beck – only the run of the water, the crying of a curlew disturbed at its nest and the champ and snort of grazing cattle. They walk out into mid-stream to eat the water dropwort, a plant highly poisonous to man. There is probably a new badger home on the sloping river-bank, half hidden in nettles; for nettles mark badger occupation just as surely as they do old human use. The sett is, however, as well guarded as any royal residence, not by the police, nor the military nor even a menacing landowner but by a large herd of inquisitive and gieversome (playful) cows. They are only too happy to join in whatever is going on but while I like cows (who does not, in reason?) they are no help at all in badger-watching. So that sett is written off. The next valley on the way home edged with pale elderflowers and wild roses seemed more promising, it had no mist and no cows – not even sheep – and only trout, jumping clear of the small pools to fall back with a gentle plop, broke the silence.

Keswick   *18 July, 1983*

Some of an old stone bank-barn high on a fell-end near here is in poor repair. Its eastern wall had a jagged crack a few years ago which was inexpertly patched up; its western one,

looking down a lake and a twisting valley to the Solway
Firth, has a multitude of gaps in its stones. Starlings are
raising young in the ones below the eaves, an ancient owl
hole in the gable has been only partially blocked and makes a
fine home for a pair of kestrels. The starlings forage amongst
the grazing cows and the hawks hunt over the uncut
hayfields and the coppice edges. All live reasonably together,
the starlings only panicking if the kestrel's flight paths and
theirs cross too nearly. The sun is on the barn all day now
and, by noon, its grey-yellow lichened stones are hot to the
hand and only the thick grass at its foot is cool and green. It
was there, gazing up at the owl hole, I almost trod on a
young, well-hidden leveret. It shot away leaving a perfect
leveret-image behind, to flatten itself again on the edge of a
patch of bright yellow bird's-foot-trefoil. Its soft little body,
its black-tipped ears laid back with a dark spot in between
and its dark eyes were all too easy to see so I gently left it. A
pregnant doe was about the barn in late spring so probably
she has other young scattered around to visit and feed –
although this one was happily eating white clover later in the
afternoon. Hares are scarce here now.

Keswick   29 August, 1983

There has been less rain this summer in the Lake Country
than in the Eden Valley to the east below the Pennines, and
the garden at Acorn Bank, a National Trust property south
of Penrith, emphasises the difference. Today's early warmth
drew the last of the dew from the grass, the last of the
night-scent from the nicotianas and opened more yellow
flowers on the clematis along the outer wall of the herb
garden. All the bricks in the garden are old, handmade, and
they soak up the sun and give back waves of herb-scent in the
inner garden. The honey bees were out early, too, and
someone will get a good hive-harvest. Inside the arch is a tall
stand of red orache (planted after the cutting winter of 1981–
2) making a foil for violet and blue plants – pale mallow, blue
chicory and flax and the stronger blues of hyssop and viper's
bugloss. Lavenders are in bloom amongst other grey-green
useful things, all set off against the yellows of elecampane,
dyer's-greenweed, fleabane, anthemis and curry plant.
Culinary plants, like differing mints and thymes, have their

places but the garden has many rarities, too. I have only seen the feathery flowers and leaves of gillenia (bowman's-root) here and in the botanic garden at Oslo. The President's garden at St John's College in Oxford has (or had?) false-dittany (the 'burning bush' which can give off an inflammable gas) and so too has Acorn Bank. The Trust, last autumn, were deeply worried about the garden – could they afford to keep it or must it lapse? However, people gave generously then, and there is a breathing space now of two years. It is not a long time but surely people will continue to appreciate the garden's near-irreplaceable quality?

Keswick *18 June, 1984*

There is no real darkness in these northern June nights when sunset glow and moonlight stretch out into first light. Today, very early, a cool air came to stir the leaves and the lengthening catkins on the birch tree outside my window. A robin began to sing quietly to itself: time to be out. The meadows in the vale were soaking with dew at that hour of the morning, the sheep feeding but the lambs not yet wanting to play. I went over the stream on a high-arched stone bridge and a faint track across the fields to join the half-forgotten bridleway below the Rigg. It must have been much used in other times, passing the small barn and ruins of Sosghyll, the fallen walls of Howgate (once an inn) and Recka (Rake How) burned down by a green-hay fire long ago. It curves, leisurely, up the fell to the small church of St John-in-the-Vale, not in any vale but on a hause between two valleys and serving both. 'Carrying' funerals used this green road, and an old farmer used to point out flat stones at intervals where they could be rested. Howgate was a natural 'resting place'; especially on the way home, Cumbrian funerals tend to be seldom totally solemn. The church is said to be on the site of a chapel belonging to the Knights Hospitallers in the thirteenth century, and once had an inn, too. I found myself smiling, wandering in the wet grass between the gravestones, remembering so many happy friends and one especially who, on being told that her father was buried just outside the inn step, remarked cheerfully, 'They've put father on t' wrong side.'

Keswick

A sprained ankle is of little use to a Country Diarist – down off the fells, not driving a car, but at least it is a good time to be idle with soft fruit over, apples unripe and time to look at things which might normally get overlooked. There is a feeling of autumn in the air and a freshness lost since early summer. Many days begin with silent mist blotting out all but the nearest trees. The early sun is only a silver orb in mist, its light catches in the dewed cobwebs on the grass and it was on such a morning lately that a fox-coloured, white-patterned spider drifted her line from the yellow clematis to a column of cypresses across the path. The outline of the web was finished and now she was working from the hub outwards making her perfect cobweb pattern. Her feet are slightly oily so she moved neatly, attaching each thread to its line with a dab from her rear before reaching for the next. It was mid-morning before the web was complete and by mid-afternoon all but the frame of it was gone and the spider quiescent on the cypress. So I moved with the sun to a baulk of timber between golden-rod and buddleia, between hoverflies and butterflies. The female butterflies, slightly darker and stockier than the males, fed assiduously on the golden flowers unruffled by the males who paused abruptly in rapid flight and mated with no time wasted. Theirs seemed the only action in this hot and scented garden, where even the butterflies drowsed.

Mungrisdale

I went back recently to the small ruined house to see again its half-fallen stone staircase and its doorless stone bake-oven. The ash trees, bare five weeks ago, are green now and not only with leaves but with the darker green mop-heads of ash keys. The sheep and their growing lambs drowsed in the sun. I think, with the help of others, I may know a little more about the house now. It was lived in until about sixty years ago and an old local lady still calls it simply, 'the Howe'. Flaska and Grisedale Commons flank opposite sides of the A66, a partly Roman road, and various 'Howes' are on the Mungrisdale side. It is of a much earlier date than Far Howe, Near Howe and Under Howe Farm, which it faces at some distance, and I think it may be the original Grisedale Howe by reason of its age. My interest in it was kindled on being told that John Slee (1559–1629) of Grisedale Howe had a son, also John, born at 'the Howe' about 1615 and, when George Fox visited nearby Mosedale in 1653, a meeting was held 'in the house of John Slee in Mungrisdale'. That meeting so fired John the second that he became 'the Eloquent Quaker' and one of the Valiant Sixty who went south from what is now Cumbria, witnessing. He and others reached Reigate in Surrey and prepared the meeting there for Fox's coming later in 1655. The local parish registers have many Slees from 1559 onwards: Sle, Sleigh, Sley, and Slee from Grisdell, Mungrisdale and Grisedale. There is no certainty but the little house, so peaceful in its age, looks as if it may have seen history in the making.

Keswick   14 July, 1986

I went on a perfect summer morning lately to a road I have not seen for many years and found it almost unchanged – but why should it have changed? After all it now peters out on the open fell, has no obvious use and only serves a few farms on its way. Look carefully, however, and you will see its past. It was always a walking road, a road for carts or for pack-horses bringing wool from the eastern fells for a mill some miles down the valley. Sometimes it was a 'carrying' road from dwellings to churchyard and those flat stones, raised from the ground, must have rested many burdens. The land below falls away steeply to the river-valley but rises even more steeply up the fell-breast above. Its upper hedge is old and varied with a line of haphazard boulders along inside setting the boundaries of small fields. They are only lightly grazed now and the turf is sprinkled with showers of white daisies and patches of red clover, buttercups and sky-bright speedwell. Shade trees – something lost from newer roads – were planted long ago and still give pools of shadow. Oak, ash and thorn, all typical north-country trees, have lime, sycamore and a true Scots pine for company. Two larches, a little apart, have all the air and space they want so one is tall, trailing long branches earthwards but the other is smaller, stouter, making a neat green umbrella. All this is no statement that things were better once – they were not, just different. Time has taken away the ring of horseshoes but it has also taken the horseflies and the clouds of smaller flies rising from warm dung.

Keswick

There is still sometimes a chill in the air but when the sun shines that chill serves only to burnish the colours further and add depth to the many greens on the oaks along the valley. These range from light green through an almost bronze-green to a yellow shine only outdone by the buttercup flowers on the tree peonies. The high rocks of Walla Crag look hard and austere where the flood of green has not reached them yet. Last month's warmth fetched a rush of bumble-bees, more than usual, and queen wasps were home-hunting, too. Small white butterflies followed and soon orange-tipped ones – but no honey bees. There are few yet, even on the apple blossom, and some local beekeepers are anxious after the last two bad summers and winters. There will be no gooseberries big enough for gooseberry plate-cakes this Whitsuntide, I think. They are almost a tradition here and once were expected to be ready for when the beekeepers began their Saturday afternoon visits to each other's hives. The stocks were gone through, discussed and even requeened, but the tea was the thing. The last spot visited saw to that, and one farm under Catbells was well known for its gooseberry plate-cake, eaten outside if the sun shone, with scalding tea and a fine view up Newlands. It was not all bees – newcomers got to know local enthusiasts' names, often new ones to them. One, on being told 'Graves', asked was it an old, a common, one, and got the reply: 'Aye, there've been Graves in Newlands since the Black Death.' And who could argue?

Isel
27 June, 1987

Someone said to me recently, talking of a long-dead friend, 'She always had time,' meaning time for other people, for their joys and sorrows. I thought of her lately on a rare, sunny July morning when I went slowly down the valley of the river Derwent enjoying the tall spotted orchids, the red ragged-robin and the blue field-geranium along a side road when I met a small procession. First, well ahead came a watchful sheepdog, then a fine black and white cow grazing along with its new, wobbly-legged calf at its side – and last of all, the farmer, barely moving. They were taking their time and I had to come to look again at another face of time in the hollow where the small church at Isel sleeps in its now green and flowery graveyard. The sun was hot on its south wall, picking out each patch of lichen – grey-white, yellow and orange – and sharpening up the lines of the three sandstone faces of 'mass tiles' (sundials) grouped beside a window about eight feet from the present ground level. All are old and weathered, the sandstone set on slate, and each has a centre hole from which the lines for the hours radiate. Only one has twenty-four (and a north indicator), the next marks the hours from 9 a.m. to 3 p.m. while the third has only four lines. They were set here in 1876 but are of pre-clock time and are still called mass tiles locally because a bent twig, stuck in the centre hole, could tell, simply, the hour of the next mass. That day the grasshoppers sang, too, to tell the sunny hours.

*Enid
J. Wilson's*
COUNTRY
DIARY

Autumn

Keswick

Last night the full moon rose to the east over the shoulder of
the hill, clear and very big, as the yellow light died in the
west. At the zenith one star swung in a pool of clear sky as a
joining point between the radiance in the east and the light in
the west. The sky was not all clear: soft white clouds and
darker masses below flying across the face of the moon gave
it a ring of silver fading to grey and warming again to gold.
The oak trees on the ghyllside looked very black and the field
of kale below cast its own shadows across the path. The geese
discovered this field of kale about a month ago and went
daily to feed there, returning at dusk. The man who owns
them walked up the fell one evening to meet their homeward
march and, to his astonishment, saw them coming down
very fast and quite silent. First came the old goose, then the
nine young ones in a compact line and, last of all, the strong
old gander. On they came hurrying, direct and arrow-
straight. As he waited under the trees he saw a fox cub
snaking along behind them, creeping very low on the
ground, cutting in from side to side and herding them as well
as any sheepdog could. As they passed, it saw him and
slipped into the wood, no doubt with a watering mouth for a
quarry it just dared not tackle. Last night the geese were
gone, the foxes not to be seen, and only a hunting owl, as
pale as moonlight and as silent, went along the woodside and
down the ghyll.

Keswick

It was bitterly cold last night with the first snow of winter
lying on the top of Scafell. A chill wind bent the dying
bracken on this piece of fell where some hardy cattle live with
the sheep. It will be interesting to see if they have any effect
on the bracken for, long ago in the Highlands, one head of
cattle used to be kept with every twenty head of sheep and
the continual bruising by the cattle-hooves would bleed the
bracken stalks and weaken them. But this bracken was a
comfort; it stood waist-high about the badgers' setts and
gave shelter from the wind. It is a long time since I watched
at this sett and as one badger emerged and went off to hunt
from the lower hole a fine animal came to the mouth of the

upper one and paused. Although every shift of the wind, or of my feet, had made a rustle it came towards me with astonishing silence, passed by me and went up the hill, snouting along the ground and in the bracken roots. Its coat was very sleek and neat, every hair lying in place from its dark head to its pale, stumpy tail. When it was about twenty yards past a low 'psst' from me brought it down to its hole again, where it backed in for a moment in a characteristic attitude of watching. Then, quite confidently, it slid downhill, jumped over the lower hole, scratched a little in the earth and went into the thick fern below on its way, no doubt, to the water meadows near the river. I found a wasps' nest down there recently half dug up, and the grubs gone – obviously the work of a badger.

Keswick   30 October, 1952

A gale blew through the early days of this week, whipping the surface of the lake, chasing spray and rain together high towards the hills. Now the wind has fallen and the lake is a sullen sheet of grey. It is still very cold outside but indoors all is snug and warm. The beemaster sits at the big table in his honeyroom surrounded by a happy clutter of half-filled honey jars and deep drums of solid honey. Down one wall hang his prize tickets, against another totters a pile of section racks, and at his feet is a drift of dry bracken to fill the tops of his hives and keep them warm through the winter. He is girt about with a vast apron, a 'brat' we call it, and slowly, with great deliberation, he puts the finishing touches to his jars. A thin old spoon is kept for visitors that they may taste the various flavours of his honey: of spring flower honey; of honey blended from gorse, heather and willow herb, but perhaps best of all the pure heather honey, smooth as cream and palely gold – the imprisoned spirit of a heathery Cumberland fell. The bees are mostly settled for the winter now. For food they have their own honey and sometimes sugar syrup too. 'When I was a lad,' says the beemaster, 'father med me fill laal troughs with sugar an' water for t'bees, but he gev 'em more. He'd fill a pudden basin with brown sugar, mash it down hard and put on t'top o' t'skep. He nivver hung'erd nor lost his bees!' In this warm room the happy days of summer are remembered, and all the backaches, the lost swarms, and the stings are forgotten. It is at those moments that a spectator's voice so often says, 'How nice to have all that honey,' but now the voice, too, is remembered and it rings true.

Keswick 4 September, 1953

On the west side of Thirlmere there rises from the roadside a row of six silver fir trees – veritable grenadiers of trees, proud and tall. Many people admire them in passing, as well they may for these are some of the finest trees in the district, but not so many people perhaps know of the seventh silver fir which stands above and behind them on the fell. This is known affectionately round here as the Giant Tree and when it was last measured in 1951 it was 128 feet tall and 128 years old. It has an enormous girth and deeply fissured bark; one of its branches, as thick as the trunk of an ordinary tree, stands out at a right angle, brushing the young growth of alder beside it. On the steep hillside halfway between the lower row and the upper giant is a curious man-made platform of earth about eight yards across and roughly circular. It has been built up at the edge with stones, now embedded in the roots of six beech trees which hug the earthen ring. These are old trees, too, and are in no way dwarfed or overborne by their lordly neighbours. It is said that the ring was used for cockfighting long ago; perhaps it was – any convenient venue would do for that – but perhaps, too, it was a favourite viewpoint for someone who lived at the old house of Armboth which stood, not far away, beside the lake.

Keswick 7 October, 1953

A few days ago, on a golden afternoon when the autumnal stillness lay like a cloak over the mountains, I found a road I have never seen before, and I shall not go that way again for fear of destroying a spell it laid on me. The road winds along a fold in the fell; it is overhung by trees, and the tall brome grasses on its banks lean inwards over the track. Some way along it stands an old house. It is flat-fronted with a stone lintel over the porch on either side of which, above and below, are blank windows looking on to a cobbled space which is partly enclosed by two swallow-haunted barns. The cobbles have grown green with grass, and along the house front in a tangle of rose bushes and low herbs grows a glory of scarlet bergamot – the finest bergamot I have ever seen. The place looked quite forsaken; the open door sagged on its hinges, dust lay on the flagged floor but a coat hung moving in the draught along the wall, so I raised my hand and knocked. From a door in the passage came an old woman, as grey as a badger but very upright and keen of eye with the soft remote voice of one who lives much alone. 'Yes,' she said, 'my bergamot – it's very bonny and it's none so common – it has been here ever since I can remember.' It seemed quite natural, in that place, that we, as strangers, should talk of her bergamot and part with a smile knowing no more of one another, and the spell is with me still. It echoes a recollection of a Victorian child's book, 'My mother says there's nothing like red bergamot . . . She says it's a deal more refreshing than old man, and not so common . . . and my Aunt Nancy she says so too!'

Keswick   29 October, 1954

The floods are slow to subside, and a waste of water lies between Derwentwater and Bassenthwaite Lake, where cormorants sit on the fence posts and mallards sail over the abandoned hayfields. Small fish jump in the shallow water, and three herons who have followed them in from the lake stand motionless by the hour, ready to spear them or any unwary vole who moves in the half-submerged tussocks. Last night, in the growing darkness, I picked my way along the flooded track to the farm, conscious of a lake on my right where the meadow usually lies and the sound of water all about me. As I rounded the curving wall I was greeted by splashes, swishing water, loud quacking, and an oath. I could only just make out the farm cats on the wall; a shadowy figure stood beside the flood; another who waded knee-deep in its middle, and the drake from the farm who sailed round and round regardless of the darkness, of the foxes who haunt the screes, and of anyone's wishes but its own. Every time it was within catching distance it submerged hurriedly and came up further away, quacking indignantly, its tail a fan of temper.

The catching took a long time, but eventually it was carried back to the farm at the head of a damp procession. The farmer's wife brought up the rear – 'Daft thing,' she said, 't'duck's bin home since darkenin', but t'drake has nea sense. Ivvery mornin' since t'field's bin flooded he won't stop for his breakfast but he's off to t'watter. He mun bide abed tomorrow.' But I wonder if he did.

Keswick   *31 August, 1955*

Signs of autumn are everywhere – in the glow of the heather on the fells and the numbers of golden fronds among the bracken, in the crying of the curlews across the night sky and the movement of small birds by day. The wet weather has made the wasps sleepy and slow, but not the hedgehog who nightly patrols the garden to see what he can find. Milk is always left for him, and a scatter of grubs from a destroyed wasps' nest was much to his liking. He found the first lot below the bush where the nest had been, but when a whole layer had been found in the branches and laid ready for his visit he came and picked each grub out of its paper case, eating them as daintily as an actress with a bunch of grapes. Hedgehogs have many uses, as I learnt at a farm where a few cockroaches frequent the warm hearth in which a fire burns summer and winter. 'There's nowt now to what there was when we fust came here,' said the farmer's wife. 'There was hundreds until Fadder tell't us what to do: "Thee mun git a laal hedgehog, lass, one that 'ull grow; put it into t'dairy – by daytime it mun sleep under t'copper."' And so it did, but when dusk fell it was out from under the boiler, across the flagged passage, and hard at work by the hearth. 'You could hear t'cranching all ower t'kitchen, an' t'laal thing grew terrible fast.' I think my hedgehog is underprivileged – no cockroaches, only milk and an occasional treat of wasp grubs.

North Westmorland 12 October, 1955

Every turn of the rough mountain road brings a different prospect – the valley peaceful in pale sunshine, the waterfall at the dale head, two whitewashed cottages with iron-studded doors, and then the road dips for the last time, crosses a noisy beck, and rises steeply round a small hill where hazels and damson trees overhang the walls. Here, high up at the end of the road, is the farm. It is very small and very old. The man who built it not only had an eye for beauty but he found the one flat place for far around; into it he fitted the house and the barns with room over for a small garden and two yew trees. I had gone to look for a bee-house, and as I laid my hand on the garden gate below two entwined rowan trees, I knew the place was untenanted. The flagged path led up to the porch, four windows in the white-washed walls looked at me but not in an inimical way. There were old-fashioned rose bushes, spearmint, and pale Michaelmas daisies beside the path and over the bee-house grew a shining bay tree. As I brushed past it to peer into the windows I was washed with waves of spice and sweetness. I do not know who lived here; no doubt in its long history the house has known good years and bad, birth and death, and maybe even tragedy, but it has such a friendly air, such an air of common goodness, that I half expected to see smoke in the cold chimneys, to hear voices in the empty rooms, or the soft stamp of cows in the deserted byres, and I think the new tenants will feel as welcome as I did.

Grasmere 11 October, 1956

The upper Rydal path from White Moss Tarn above Grasmere to Rydal Mount is not a busy place at any time, and now in the gold of autumn its beauty is deepened and enriched by quietness. The warm colours of the dying grass beside the tarn; the red and gold of chestnut and hazel; the birches looking as Dorothy Wordsworth saw them in this place over 150 years ago, 'like large golden flowers', are set among the varying greens of moss and stone. The hazel nuts are ripe and fall in showers from their cups. Halfway along the path a dry-stone waller is at work in the oak wood and his liquid whistle and the clink of his hammer on stone echoing through the rocks and trees could easily belong to some gnome or troll left over from other times. He has, too, a spare, brown look, a cheerful red face, a glint in his eye, and the readiness to talk which people often have whose working life is passed in loneliness. The wall was smashed by what he calls a 'cobble' – a rock of immense size which fell from the crag in spring, crushing bushes and scarring trees, and lying now in raw ugliness among the fern. Not many people follow his trade nowadays; it needs much skill to settle a wall's foundation, lay the 'throughs' – stones which go from side to side of the walls – and to finish the top with overlapping slabs.

Keswick   12 September, 1958

These misty, gentle mornings are the epitome of early autumn. Blue smoke rises vertically from the farms, the mountains are half-hidden in cloud, and sounds carry far across the valley in the still air. The hedges in the lane which leads down to the lake-marsh are tangled with honeysuckle, pale flowers and scarlet berries both together, with the heavy heads of ripening haws, green crab-apples and elder leaves which show the first hint of autumn purple. The stooks of corn in the fields lean damply and rather drunkenly together, and six magpies are gathered in a little knot on the stubble until first one, then two, and then all rise fluttering in the air. They strike at one another with wings and feet outthrust, more like gamecocks than magpies; their severe black and white loses its severity here against the golden stubble and is gay and lively. Their clattering voices mix with the other morning sounds: a clucking hen, a heron on its way to the lake, and the sound of running water. There is a very old ash tree near the river; its upper branches are mouldering away, riddled by goat-moths and woodpeckers, and its trunk is just a hollow shell. Out of its roots a runnel of decayed earth and owl pellets spreads into the grass; not one owl but many, indeed generations of owls must be responsible for so many pellets. They are made up of fur, little bones and skulls of mice, shrews, and voles, and some of the skulls still have the orange teeth characteristic of these small rodents. Everything – trees, grass, and hedges – is hung with dew-soaked cobwebs.

Keswick *23 September, 1958*

At seven o'clock this morning the sky was full of swallows; scores of them were silhouetted in flight against the turbulent sky driven by a westerly wind. They have been here lately at first light and in the late afternoon, but soon they will all have gone. The salmon are coming strongly up the river and with the water in half-flood they are getting easily up the side of the weir and not being dashed back as they so often are. But perhaps the best indication of the time of year is the fact that Champ – the eight-year-old foxhound – is no longer to be seen at the farm. Hunting started about a fortnight ago, but it is at present mainly a question of getting the young dogs into ways and getting the fat off the older ones who – like Champ – have spent a comfortable summer at a farm. Champ has visited the kennels throughout the summer when the spirit moved him, the four-mile walk down the vale being a nice little outing, but he has always come back and has been at hand to help campers with leftovers – or anything else they have left lying about. Lately he has been camped out away from the farm beside a dead sheep, not allowing any other dog to approach.

No one came to fetch him for the hunt, nothing – except some internal clock – told him the time, and yet this time he has gone and not returned. It will take a little time, some exercise, and a 'dose of wemmel' (hungering) before he is much of a menace to a healthy fox.

Keswick *7 November, 1958*

Many of the stone circles which used to exist in this country were uprooted long ago and one of my books says that of one circle only two stones remain beside the present village; I went to look for them once on a bright, blowy day. The farmer on whose land I proposed to wander was most co-operative. He had never heard of the circle but he told me that a line of standing stones down one side of his land and another a quarter of a mile away marked village rights of way for cattle to go to water. Many years ago someone tried to close the way but there was a village meeting, a throwing down of fences, and the beasts may still go that way. The first line of stones is of a kind of limestone, the coral and the shell shapes in it showing pink and polished as smooth as soapstone where the animals have rubbed. An old man came to watch me and to give advice. He spoke of half-forgotten people, of 'Fighting Mac', a 'terrible laal tag-rag of a fellow', who used to sit at the roadside, wearing black glasses, and breaking stones for road-mending. When he was set to split an unusually large pile he would spread broken stones neatly over the top and leave the rest. He talked, too, about a farm across the valley which has been owned by the same family for time out of mind. Three generations live there now; there is Old Tom, Young Tom, and Tom-among-t'-Bairns, and Young Tom is 'wearing' his second wife. I know no more about the stone circle than I did, but a lot more about other things.

Keswick   20 October, 1960

The darkness seems to come down suddenly and very solidly in these late October days; there has been low cloud and mist on the hills and in the valleys for several days. Heavy showers of rain drown the daylight early. Everything was very quiet at the farm this evening after the lamps were lit: the dogs were silent in the barn, wearied no doubt by a long day on the fell collecting sheep; the terrier on the hearth-rug before the fire barely stirred in her sleep and even the fire burned quietly with no wind in the chimney to draw it into life. This silence gave a comfortable air to the conversation, an idle 'crack' full of ruminative pauses and digressions about people and places, but especially about people, for here – where so many are related by blood, or marriage, or both – there is plenty to talk about. How would you describe a woman who can never stop talking? Here she is a 'three-ha'penny rattle', a 'bletherskite', or even a 'chitterwallit', but does not really deserve criticism. Criticism is reserved for one who is a 'hard-feaced un', 'a proper boilin' bit' (remembering knuckle-ends of ham) whose face 'wad spoil a pick'. How much happier to be labelled 'that nice, old-fashint folk', or to be like the man who lives on the other side of Skiddaw. He is dumpy, shiny-apple cheeked, and smiling and is said to be a 'cheerful laal beggar, he shines like a closet door on a frosty morning'.

Solway Firth   5 October, 1962

The north Cumberland coast seems an empty, deserted place
on this October morning with the tide far out across the
scaurs of the Solway Firth, but a closer look shows how
unreal this seeming emptiness is. Party after party of small
birds – mostly larks – are migrating south along the
foreshore, urged on by the cool northerly air, and the local
skylarks, possibly feeling their territory threatened, attack
them fiercely as they pass, singing with renewed vigour after
each sally. The coast was scoured by the recent gales, and the
turf of the foreshore is fresh and green; the leaves of the
burnet rose are darkly crimson but in one place I found a
spray of frail and almost scentless roses. There is some sea
thrift still in flower and a little thyme, and, where the turf
gives place to marram grass, the sea holly is almost over, but
still keeps a flush of brilliant blue in its smaller leaves.

   Again, where the grass gives place to sand, the saltwort is
strongly green and the sea-rocket has violet flowers, but
nothing has more colour than the small shingle, damp with
dew, between the highest tide wrack and the usual tideline. It
has been gathered by the sea from both sides of the Solway
and is of every shade from palest amber to black. The gulls
are asleep in the sun far out on the firm sand, but the curlews,
oystercatchers, and redshanks are all in search of food, and
already in the sand and the rocks there is that almost
imperceptible murmur which comes as the tide begins to run
in. One must always remember that this is a place, so
innocent seeming, where the tide has always been said to
'come in like a galloping horse'.

Rydal Lake   31 October, 1963

Sometimes some small happening, or set of happenings, will
turn a time and a place upside down and make things seem
out of joint. It was so for me by Rydal Lake one day this
week on a perfect, still October afternoon when the plumy-
headed reeds nodded softly along the lake. The willows shed
their leaves gently and one could hear a party of coots –
sounds travel far now – making cheerful, watery splashings
where the river runs in, but the traffic – buses, cars and
lorries – bustled purposefully past, oblivious, by necessity, of

the beauty round them. In a long pause in the traffic a quite different sound began; it was the quiet honking of wild swans and there, in the still water, was a pair of whooper swans, the first of the winter. Maybe this was their first journey south on migration, for these most lovely of birds, immaculate and majestic, were very ill at ease. They sailed round one another, murmuring, bowing their heads and bending their long necks in a kind of swan-ballet but keeping very close to one another. One could imagine that they wondered what this small piece of water, edged with noise, could be. Suddenly, they had had enough and rose together, their dangling feet making spurts of white water as they went, to wheel up and over the fell. I saw them again a little later, dark against the evening sky over Easedale, and hoped that they would find water to their liking somewhere, or that other swans, more used to the present disquiet, would join them from the north. After all, swans must have come to Rydal before man did.

Keswick   19 October, 1964

The foxhounds – seldom so-called here, but more often referred to simply as 't'dogs' – have been back in the kennels for some weeks now from the farms where they have been 'walked' during the summer and are getting in trim for a hard winter's work on the fells. Many of the old hands are ready to go when the time comes; indeed one hound – Champ, who used to spend his summers near Helvellyn – did not need to be fetched, he just went on his own. He was an independent beast, anyhow, and well known far and wide. He went for walks with visitors until they had eaten their lunch, and robbed tents, being particularly partial to bacon and cheese, which he sometimes shared with the farm terrier. The only thing he hated was being bathed. This very seldom happened – only before show days – and once after he was bathed for Rydal Show he just took off and disappeared. The old man who was to show him was most upset seeing his promised outing fading as well as his half of the winnings (if any). However, the farmer's wife knew Champ and left a dish of bones below her bedroom window and sure enough in the dark early hours there he was, crunching away. So Champ and his friend got to Rydal after all but there was no prize that year for so bedraggled a hound. He was greeted with some surprise too by a man from the next valley, over the immense ridge of Helvellyn. 'Well,' he said, 'Ah nivver thowt to see that beggar at Rydal today, he was walking around Patterdale yesterday afternoon.'

Keswick *17 October, 1966*

Time was when the Forest of Inglewood, the English wood, covered much of north Cumberland and even lapped at the feet of the Lake District fells. It is all gone now, the last ancient oak fell at Wragmire Bank (not far from Carlisle) in 1824 and yet that part of the county is still better wooded than the rest; it is good land for trees. However, one seldom gets the feeling of a big, old wood anywhere in Cumberland and only the legends remain of Adam Bell, Clym of the Clough, and lesser outlaws and poachers. Inglewood must have been a terror to travellers and so it had its hospices, one of which (built by the Knights Hospitallers of St John) stood on its farthest edge astride the fell-top between the Vale of St John and the Naddle Valley – probably where the church of St John now is.

There was an inn there once and, within living memory, a school. But early last Sunday morning, with the mist barely rising from the valleys, the church of St John had a feeling of complete isolation. The mist wrapped it no less than Inglewood could have done, the flames of the altar candles rose straight in the still air, and even the flowers left over from last week's Harvest Festival could not take away its air of remoteness. It was silent within but not without: the clamour of fieldfares gobbling the berries on the churchyard yews was loud and insistent. These are not old yews; nor is the church, as it stands, old. But, no doubt, yews were here long ago (Adam Bell had 'bowes and arrowes kene', maybe of yew); and fieldfares may have come here as long as trees have grown in Britain to eat and spread the berries, keeping alive a ghost Inglewood.

Buckinghamshire

If I leave the Lake District – even for a short time – there are
some places I seem to carry with me, so much are they part of
my life and of me, and often, between waking and sleeping,
the mind goes back to them. I remember, especially perhaps,
the green roads. Other people and other times give them
different names, for they were tracks, pack-horse ways,
'carrying' roads, and 'corpse' roads, too – for these were the
ways along which coffins were borne on the shoulders of
neighbours and friends, often over steep and stony places, to
some remote church. The one I know best goes from the
level of St John's Vale to the little church of St John high on
the fell. It goes through many gates, past ruined and fallen
places – cottages, garths, an inn and a farm – rising and
falling steeply, terraced along the fell. It is walled for some of
its length, and at the last farm, Rake How, where the track
rises steeply to the church, there are two sentinel yews. Rake
How was burnt down over sixty years ago when too-green
hay caught fire and, when I went there one early morning
lately, it was very quiet. Cold dew lay on the grass and the
vale was choked with mist but sun lit the mountain-tops and
the sky above was limpid blue. Tradition has it that carrying
funerals approaching Crosthwaite church (at Keswick) from
the north-east broke into the 'Old Hundredth' as they
breasted the last rise – there would, one feels, be little 'wind'
for that after Rake How. But I thought, as I rested, what a lot
we miss nowadays – the living get to, and leave, the little
church so easily but they miss the comfort (in every sense)
that this chain of ruins, Sosghyll, Howgate, Rake How and
the rest, would give.

Keswick

The weather has broken at last but it will take some time and
a lot of rain to restore the Lake District to normal after the
drought. The lakes and tarns are low, and Thirlmere – being
essentially a reservoir – shows its dryness more than most.
However, if you are interested in the bones of history,
Thirlmere's shore has much to tell now of what it was like
when there were two small lakes in the valley, not one, and
farms and cottages stood there. There were, before the

flooding in 1894, two promontories on the west side – Hawes How and Deergarth How – both are islands now, and although Hawes is not (so far as I know) ever joined to the land, Deergarth is occasionally, and at present only a thin line of water remains. At Armboth, farther north, where there was once a substantial house and outbuildings, one can see today below their ruins the line of a road along the valley and the curve of another which went over a five-spanned bridge between the lakes to Dalehead opposite. There are tree stumps, some very big, above the present low-water line, and on the site of the small farm at Nether Place there is the curve of an old retaining wall, a one-span stone bridge, and a line of bleached, grey trunks still standing, clawed into the stones. Sheep are grazing on what once was fertile fields but now they feed on a grass-like growth of isoetes, usually deep in the water, and from which sprout dry land plants – cudweed and persicaria. This shore has, for me, a strange unearthly beauty, but surely, after so long under water, its ghosts are gone – the dog with fiery eyes and the two Armboth skulls which commuted between there and Calgarth on Windermere.

Keswick   *27 October, 1969*

It is almost a matter of pilgrimage for me to go to the Newlands oak woods – Birkrigg and Keskadale in adjoining valleys – at this time of the year. These stunted oaks may be very ancient (oaks owned by the Duke of Northumberland were recorded in Newlands in 1660), and some have been coppiced long ago. It is a scramble to get to either wood, especially Keskadale, up slopes which seem to be in constant change and apt to slip under one's feet. Erosion and weather are aided by rocks and even badgers in search of cockchafers and other grubs; sheep graze the fell using the wood for shelter in winter and taking any green shoot – indeed, was it not for the anchoring oaks one feels that the steep scree-slope would quietly slip into the beck far below, as it has in places. It is the acorn crop which interests me, and this year for the first time in many it is almost abundant in restricted places – not on the wood's edge where frost, wind, and drought have full play but inside the wood where the ground is slightly better and the oaks give shelter one to another. One tree, here, is laden with maturing, sessile acorns. It is worth going to Keskadale at any time of the year but it is seldom better than now with the oaks and the lower bracken slopes changing from green to yellow, gold to russet. The wood is moss-grown with hard ferns and late bell-heather flowers in the crevices, there are fungi too – orange and the lovely violet-purple of laccaria. One is never lonely here in spite of the October quiet – rooks feed on the acorns, a buzzard hunts along the ridge, and a sparrowhawk over the valley. A Herdwick-cross sheep grazed past and paused to stare with that special sort of dumb insolence only a fell sheep and, I am told, some of the army, can produce.

Keswick 8 *November, 1971*

The autumn colours are fine this year, but not so fine as they sometimes are. A damp autumn gives little red or scarlet. But this morning I saw from the high shoulder of a fell above Derwentwater a long shaft of sunlight which cut through the clouds to touch, briefly, the wild cherries below Skiddaw Dodd. It was the only true red in all the long valley. However, the smoulder of dying bracken on the fells and the varied greens, yellows and orange throw a counterpane of colour across the mountains and the valley. Each small island on Derwentwater is studded with varying hues and the damp air and lack of sunlight (except for that one errant gleam) serve only to deepen all the colours. Autumn is a time for change and, for me, it is also the time to catch up with all the things that summer has left undone or unseen. Now is the time to begin to find out again where the otters (if any) still are. It is some time since I saw one. They have left many of their old haunts near here, mill-lades and buildings have gone; river-banks have been cleared of growth and much cover is gone. Perhaps some otters still follow the smaller becks in quieter places and it would not be surprising if they came to this beck on the fell for it is very quiet in winter. The water rushes down rock-chutes and idles in small deep pools and these are where the trout lie and herons come, too, to fish. The source of the beck lies well over a thousand feet up in the roots of a higher fell – high, you might say, for an otter. But one dark day an otter was seen fishing peacefully near where Bright Beck runs into Stickle Tarn below Pavey Ark in Langdale, and that is even higher.

Keswick

Beatrix Potter, when she wrote about Tommy Brock (the badger) and Mr Todd (the fox) living on terms of toleration – until Tommy badly overstepped the mark – was simply stating a fact about wild animals generally. Left to themselves, wild animals have their own in-built understanding. The red-deer on the fells can be seen perhaps not grazing with the sheep, but moving alongside them, foxes and badgers pass within yards of one another with no acknowledgment from either side, and rabbits sometimes live in part of a big badger sett even if a badger is in residence. I have seen a fox go through a flock of sheep with no disturbance and once I saw a badger walk, leisurely, through a field of ewes and their lambs. The sheep watched its progress but with no concern. A dog, in either case, would have caused panic. A farm horse who lived on a slope near here must have been well known to the local badgers for I watched it one evening, just at dusk, as it plodded up the mound of earth below the badger's hole just as the badger emerged to test the evening air. The badger simply ducked as the horse went over and was out again at once. Tamed animals have closer links – Sandy, the last working horse at Thirlmere, shared his field with a goat in his later years and the goat's owner said he was sure the goat thought she was a horse too. They moved, grazed, and lay down together and when the goat had kids (a very lively bunch) they made very free with old Sandy. When he lay down they leapt and slid all over his big body, using it as a climbing frame, trampoline, or even a pillow – but Sandy was ever of a patient nature.

Keswick

If you live in the middle of the Lake District, as I do, it is a pleasure but sometimes almost a necessity to get out of the rain and cloud-covered hills and look for a more open land where rain and sun can race in from the Irish Sea, fly over and be gone, unanchored by any mountain-tops. I went yesterday to the low limestone scarps which face down sea inlets to Morecambe Bay and found what I sought. These are always empty, lonely places and seldom more so than at the end of summer. June brings a flush of colour to their short turf but that is long gone now and everything is deep green, silver and white before the hand of autumn is laid on the land. The age-old junipers, thorns and yews are moulded into strange shapes by the wind off the sea and today a brisk air rippled through them. All the flowers here are small and tough, silver heads of carline thistle lie flush with the grass and there are still sprigs of thyme and yellow bed straw. The blue-purple field-gentians are in flower, but much more in keeping with this limestone land is a sprinkling of pure white gentians. They were not easy to see in the limestone clitter nor were the new white spheres of puff-balls or the mushroom caps (enough of those for supper). This is a land which belongs to falcons and today, for the hour I spent there, a kestrel hung, hunting, as patient as death – its head to the wind. It got no voles or mice while I watched but was content, at times, to drop like a stone and take beetles from cowpats. It was sadly tried by a gang of swallows, hunting too, who time and again flew straight at it and swerved off as sharply. There was peace, it seemed, for me but not for kestrels.

Keswick   21 October, 1974

Autumn is supposed to be a season of mists and mellow fruitfulness. Well, there is plenty of mist and cloud this October and the berried trees everywhere are laden. But mellow, no. It has been too wet and cold for that. The hawthorns which divide the Castle Rigg stone circle field from the ancient lane which runs along its hilltop ridge are no exception, their berries bring birds from far and wide – but autumn shows its face in many ways. The dry-stone walls, ancient too, which follow the thorns are mossed and lichened, the grey-green lichen cups, now burgeoning to their season of growth, and today a cold north wind combed through the crevices of the walls. Nothing can stop it on this open ridge. Mist and cloud, early on, almost hid the mountains from Borrowdale through Helvellyn to the rounded flanks of Saddleback and Skiddaw but slowly, with errant gleams and sudden shafts, the sun came through and the true face of autumn shone out in scarlet and yellow, orange and brown and gold. The wild cherries and the rowans, especially in the dark-gullied rocks of St John's Vale, burned with an astonishing light. That was not all. The southern end of the lane is deep-banked on either side and topped by a hedge. Both hedge and bank are lately trimmed, losing some of their wealth of fern and leaf cover but uncovering other things. There are yellow heart-shaped leaves of violets, red stems of herb-robert and turning bilberry leaves, and in and out of them all are the galleries and filling stores of mice and voles. This must be a very old hedge judged on the yardstick of one species to thirty yards implying a hundred years of growth.

Keswick   *20 September, 1976*

It seems at present, in a tempest of wind and rain, as if winter might follow hard on the heels of summer, missing autumn. Indeed, the parched fells have been autumn-brown for some time now and the dry becks, the shrinking lakes and the silent woods created if not a dead landscape certainly one in suspended animation. The migrant warblers – willow, wood and garden – slipped south early this year almost unnoticed. They usually pause and rest in this garden but not this time. The flocks of redpolls which generally come in late August have not arrived yet and in their place are hundreds of starlings who sweep round the sky in well-drilled squadrons. They are uneasy, dropping to settle on the berried rowans at the garden's edge, bending the branches to near-breaking point and, as suddenly, rising to alight in the crowns of the spruces where they sit neatly spaced out and murmuring in unison. There are starling flocks on the rowans at Thirlmere too, but Thirlmere itself is of especial interest at present to anyone with an eye to its past. The lake is still low and the land round it has gone back in time – walls which once edged roads and fields are plain to see and so, too, are the patterns of houses, barns and cottages and even the 'City' of Wythburn and the ruins of the Cherry Tree Inn on opposite shores are on dry land. It is worth noticing what plants are first to colonise the new land – redleg, water-pepper and cudweed are dominant and all are acceptable to hungry sheep. Red-deer graze along the shore in the dusk and, in this morning's wet light, a small party of Canada geese were feeding on green grass meadows where water often lies. It will take a lot of rain to alter all this.

Keswick   19 September, 1977

The heather is fading on the fells and the fields in the valley look almost unnaturally green, the fogg there is ready for another cut – indeed some fields have been cut twice already. The grassy levels by the lake have, by contrast, come early to autumn and lie open and yellow in the north wind but the path down to the river, marsh and lake is sheltered, overhung by well-ripened blackberries, rose-hips and hazel nuts so it looks like being a happy year for squirrels. It was all strangely silent this morning (the badgers had been hard at work during the night, digging) and the marshes look as if they had been scoured by showers and wind, got ready for the winter influx of birds from the north, and already there are big rafts of ducks out on the lake and a score of fishing cormorants resting on the line of posts which run out into the water. It was a morning of sudden showers and equally sudden stretches of watery blue sky; I faced the weather as I went down the marshes almost too blinded to see a rush of widgeon going overhead. The sheep here are in good fettle for amongst the yellow bents there are patches of fine green turf inundated by the river in times of flood and enriched by the silt it brings. The storm passed over as I turned back to face up the valley to where Helvellyn blocks off its eastern end, but it left long shafts of grey and silver rain hanging across the Newlands fells and their progress recalled, very clearly, a remark made to me last week by an elderly woman who once lived on a farm there. She said that the columns of rain on a wet Sunday lately passed across the face of Newlands 'like great, grey men walking'.

Keswick

When I look out over the autumn fields and woods between here and Derwentwater I know that they all have names – Green Eskham, Eskinbeck Meadow, Grassings Wood and so on – only a few of scores recorded on old maps of this valley, but there are many others with names long used and, so far as I know, written nowhere and live only in the long memories which hold them. Who, for instance, will remember Cabbage Garth below Skiddaw or Honeypot in the next valley after a few more years? Many of the names describe the use or the character of the land and are disregarded to disadvantage like the field below here, a 'bottom' which was once recorded as being 'coarse and wet, not to be ploughed but used as pasture' – tractors have often got mired down there in recent years. Some names are descriptive. Wetlands and Froth are at the top of Bassenthwaite and their neighbour is Pickle, which means a very small bit of land. There are many named in-tacks (land won from the fell) as well as garths, thwaites and closes with ewe, calf, deer and even bull labels. There is, too, a Bull Coppy where, perhaps, a bull lived or visited but a coppy here is a three-legged stool and the rock knob at the field's centre looks just like one, but turned upside down. I looked out lately from a warm farm kitchen across a green slope to Helvellyn and was told that Sleathwaite was 'the best field on the place' but there was also Laddry where the fell rose steeply from Beckside, Sidelings, Low Dale and Penny Wall. But who, I wondered, gave their names to Mary Meadow, Raynold Holm and Rob Holm? Were they the people who first built the walls and cleared the land of stones, or were they an easier living generation who came with the Great Rebuilding? Some things seem happiest left behind in the mist of time.

Keswick

16 October, 1978

This has been a difficult year for Cumbrian farmers in a land which is never easy by way of its narrow valleys and high rainfall and what has been won from the land this autumn has been in the teeth of the weather. But there is more to Cumbria than mountains and if you look north from the last rise of the fells across the Solway plain to the sea and the Scottish hills beyond you will see now a prosperous landscape. The fields on the plain (in reality a series of slopes down to the sea) have kept much of their old character with strips of varying width mostly running north and south with a patchwork of vivid green fogg, golden stubble (it is not burnt here) and blue-green roots. Today a combine harvester sat, sedate and alone, in a field corner and it made me wonder all over again how the harvest was got in bad years long ago when there were only families and horses to do it all. An old friend of mine in south Westmorland died this June. His family had been on the same farm for three hundred years. He himself belonged to an older world and often talked happily about his hard-working youth when the family threshed as a unit. Four of them, father, mother and two sons, stood in a ring round six or nine sheaves laid, heads inwards, on a raised wooden platform above the stone floor of the barn with big and smaller doors open to blow away the lighter chaff. Their flails needed to rise and fall in perfect unison – like bell-ringers striking one at a time – but he was always afraid of the task because a flail can give you a nasty clip. 'T'cat under t'lug,' he called it, and he was always glad to escape to the top of the stack and throw down the sheaves. Their implements had yew handles, as smooth as silk with age and use, and the flail proper was attached with leather, but theirs were done with eel-skin got from the huge eels in the lower streams: nothing else was so supple or so strong.

Keswick   30 October, 1978

The Carlisle to Settle railway is the highest in England as well as one of the most beautiful and difficult to build. It rises from the green Eden Valley in curves, tunnels and viaducts to over a thousand feet at the watershed near Ribble Head. There has been a lot of rain so the becks in the higher valleys are brown and full and the cattle stand muddily grouped about the barns. These at first are Cumbrian barns – bank-barns with a lower floor for the beasts and a run-up at the back for carts to the haymew above. They are mostly grouped comfortably together with houses and other buildings and, indeed, if you look down into the small village of Crosby Garrett there seems to be a bank-barn to every farm. Blea Moor, high and desolate, is empty now – no

134

curlews, few sheep, and only grassy distances and sky reflecting peat pools below the tower of Ingleborough. As the line follows the Ribble down, the landscape changes. Here there are innumerable small, neat fields intersected by limestone walls and, it seems, an isolated barn to every two or three fields. But these are not bank-barns, just smaller barns set tight to the slope at the limit of cultivation: they used to keep fodder handy for the winter and cows were milked there in summer. Why the difference? Is it simply a different farming method or are the Cumbrian barns really an inheritance from Norse settlers (there are a lot of bank-barns in Norway) who brought the pattern with them when they came?

Keswick 10 November, 1980

This is the time of year for sheep sales – all sorts of sheep, all sorts of places. Indeed, there was an unusual air of tension at a farm one day lately but it turned out that the farmer and his wife were going to the nearest mart hoping to buy a Texel ram. He had long fancied a Texel ram. So, naturally, today the first question was, 'Have you got your Texel?' No, he had not – a Suffolk, yes, but not a Texel. Marts are places for meeting old friends, having a good crack and seeing what others are up to – and this he did. He looked at a pen of five Texels with another farmer and remarked (unwisely), 'That's the one I'd buy – if I was buying.' But when the bidding came the man looked him straight in the eye, across the pen, and bought the chosen one. All is fair, it seems, in love, war and sheep sales. He will, he says, 'wait on', better luck perhaps another day.

The rain bucketed down this morning, spilling the last golden leaves from the damson trees. There was little doing outside but inside the firelight sparked off the horse brasses on the wall – hoops, crescents, circles and a small, more convoluted, set belonging to a long-dead pony. Brasses, like horseshoes, may be said to bring luck but there is always the question of how shoes should be hung. One, over the barn door here, hangs with its front up, the way a horse would walk and the vet, a Scot, says this is correct. A second, however, hangs over the byre and its front is down, cup-like, to hold in the luck – that is the Cumbrian way. No chances are being taken, one or other must be right.

Keswick

September is a chancy time to go looking for badgers.
Mating can go on from August to October and so there is a
lot of visiting and moving about going on as well as
refurbishing old homes and establishing new ones. A pile of
discarded bedding lies outside the sett on the bluff above the
mountain beck where the afternoon sun filters down through
thin tree cover. Badgers have been flipping cowpats over in
the water-meadows in search of food – no other creature does
it so neatly – so it seemed worth going back just before dusk.

Meanwhile, it was the swallows' afternoon. They kept to
the course of the beck, a score hovered round the green
crown of a waterside ash getting flies, some over flowered
rush-heads – perhaps taking rush-moth larvae. Most of the
young are now adept in flight but several rested on fence rails
or on the warm track. The main body, however, swept low
along the fast-flowing beck, pitching with wing-tips
touching, momentarily, to drink in passing. Later,
everything had changed – no birds and no sound except of
water. Things seemed right for badgers.

A knee-high mist lay along the fields, a small breeze blew
from the sett and the moon was taking the sun's place. The
cows who, lately, were giddy, over-playful and inquisitive
are become staid matrons with not a kick between them and
so darkness came and thicker dew – but no badgers. Perhaps
the night and the place are reward enough? There may be
other nights, if none so lovely.

Keswick

It gets more difficult as the years go by to see what the face of
the land, of the lower fells, was like in times past. Land goes
into different use and farm buildings fall leaving only some
slight indication of their existence – say, columbines on an
empty moor or a morello cherry tree in a wall corner on
Helvellyn's side. I sat this morning on a slab of Skiddaw slate
high up in one of its ghylls, with the bracken turning to
bronze and the sun drawing the mist up from the fields.
Thirty years ago this place showed from the valley as a series
of deeply terraced fields in a green oblong below the heather.
The terraces have always been a puzzle. It is said that they

were brought into cultivation in the corn shortage of the Napoleonic wars. Certainly, 'tatie haver' – many-headed oats used for haver bread – was grown at much the same height on Whinlatter Pass across the valley. The outline of the farm is still here – piles of Skiddaw stone from its walls, Borrowdale slates from its roof, and a fine Borrowdale gate-post lie in the rushes and nettles. The terraces are being swallowed by the bracken, but what turf remains is some of the finest on the fell, starred in summer with heartsease and now with the frilled faces of eyebright. A month ago there were mushrooms, too. Two tall elms stand above the gate-post and, at the foot of one, an owl's feather stirs gently – so the place is not wholly deserted.

North Cumbria *26 September, 1983*

I like to get out of the mountains sometimes, to push the horizons back into longer distances and wider plains and to see, too, another view back into history on the face of the land. All four points of the compass are visible today from this high Border land north of the Roman Wall with, at least, four differing sorts of weather in a constant changing of colour, clear sky and cloud. There is a lowering sky to the south which can suddenly lift and leave like a distinct line of Cumbrian tops – Helvellyn, Saddleback, Causey Pike, amongst lesser fells. Christianbury Crags are dark to the north-east, as dark as the conifers below them – are there still 'wild' goats up there? The squared-off top of Birrenswark is brighter to the north-west – a place which has had Celtic deities, crowned goddess and horned god – as well as Roman roads and fort. There is sun in the west over Criffel barred with diagonals of rain, and the Solway Firth between the lands is a pure and shining silver arm stretching into the sea plains. But what of the land at one's feet? It is greener than at home and the fields are often divided with earth and stone lykes topped by hedges or by lines of old beeches which may have been hedges, too, once. The beeches are heavy with mist, the hazels with nuts and there are big herds of cattle in the fields. At this time of the year, before the railway age, there may have been just as many for this is where some of the great Scottish drove roads, still marked with wide green verges and night stopping places, crossed the Border bound for autumnal English markets.

Keswick   *8 October, 1984*

Today was just an ordinary autumn day, one of sunshine and cloud, but after midday the sun got the better of the mist. Bumble-bees and Red Admiral butterflies came to feed on the pale mounds of heath in bloom beside the birdbath and the butterflies stayed on to bask, half asleep, in the warmth. Tonight is not an ordinary night at all however – but a night with a different dimension and one to remember. The brown owls have come right up to the wide-open, curtained windows and are probably in the birch outside. I shall not stir the curtains. Perhaps it is an owl family for their range of sound covers everything from confiding chirrups to full-throated owl cries. My cat is out, too, and I cannot but wonder what his part is in the darkness. He is a silent hunter and can turn his face almost full circle and will sit, prick-eared, listening to the mice below the sill and his eyes, round, dark and very full-orbed, are 'owl' rather than 'cat' – indeed an owl without wings. The sky was barred with cloud at sunset but now it is clear and cold, almost a frost sky with only half a moon and the stars glittering as they do in frost. The bats were here earlier, at dusk, and hunting assiduously, perhaps laying up resources for the cold to come. So, so long as the owls do not 'call my name', it will long be a night to remember – but not perhaps for some moths and some mice, with bats, owls and cats all seeming to conspire against them.

Keswick   *22 October, 1984*

It is quite difficult to reconcile the magpies of spring, the scourge of the woodlands, with the same birds now – the acrobats and comedians of the garden. I suspected that they had raised a brood in the dark spruces below the hedge, but now it looks like two, or perhaps two separate families have combined into a magpie mafia who come and go, usually ten together and sometimes eleven. They enjoy the pickings on the lawn and especially the funguses. Twenty years ago a daughter of the house got interested in fungus, brought some home to identify, and threw them out. They have thrived ever since. I wondered what was taking some of the funguses and oversetting the rest – the magpies, of course. They plane down from the spruces in ones and twos until all are present, strutting, chatting, and menacing one another. They like boletuses (scaber and edulis), they simply shred the white caps off any russulas, but it is the scarlet, white-spotted caps of fly agarics they go for avidly. Today a junior bird got away with a whole cap, holding it in its beak like a riot-shield against the other birds.

Perhaps a flight of black and white, long-tailed and spread-winged magpies look their best silhouetted against the shining golds and yellows of the Borrowdale fells. The first redwings of the winter came over, high and wild, on 7 October, but today they, too, are in the garden, sometimes overbalancing on the sprays of orange-berried rowans, sometimes righting themselves with a flash of bright underwing. There are no berries for jelly left on that tree – it was stripped in forty minutes.

Keswick
20 October, 1985

October is not like any other month. The year may be on the decline but October days often have a feeling of hope, of next year's promise and, indeed, to live in the country is to learn that there is always another year. There was a cool breeze this afternoon and everything glittered with recent rain and present sun. A wide shining rainbow lay along the ridge below Skiddaw and its colours were unearthly bright and made more so by a backcloth of wet, red bracken. The green fields in the next valley seemed almost unnaturally green where they sloped down to the twisting silver ribbon of the beck which overflowed the marshy fields from Toad Pots (well named) to Mosses' Corner. The sun struck flashes of light from the wet rocks of Gait Crag and from Helvellyn's end. A few thunderheads still rose and lingered over the Pennines but here – overhead – the sky was clear and of an almost unfathomable blue, almost beyond the grasp of mind or eye, the sort of sky which gives meaning to infinity. Then – almost imperceptibly at first – the lower sky was alive with small, fast-moving dots which became swallows in a whirling concourse, dipping briefly over the farmyard. It was gone as suddenly as it had come. Three solid ravens, not to be outdone, tumbled, twisting from the blue over Wanthwaite End. The swallows, passing, marked the end of their year; the ravens, playing, tell of the one to come.

Enid J. Wilson's COUNTRY DIARY

Winter

Keswick

29 December, 1950

A full moon is still very important in the country as many of the hunt balls and village 'dos' are arranged for then. As the old molecatcher crossed the farmyard the other evening he glanced at the sky and remarked: 'Aye, t'parish lamp's lit,' and sure enough there was the full moon rising brightly over Bull Cop. It was the night of the Hunt Ball. It reminded me of Bottom enjoining his company to 'find out moonshine' for the time of their play. The old molecatcher visits the farms, but the young son at this farm has his own very successful methods. I am told that a long bramble put into the mole's run will tangle in its fur and make it an easy victim, but have never tried the method myself. One which he brought into the farm kitchen hissed most furiously and tried to dig its way into the flagged floor. The farm cat catches moles, but how she does it is a mystery.

Many of the wild creatures take advantage of moonshine, too; there was a heavy scent of fox in the early morning in the gorse thicket on the hill. It is infested with rabbits and such small deer and is a happy hunting ground for foxes. The gorse buds are swelling fast and there are one or two golden flowers already.

Keswick

16 November, 1951

The mist was rising in long skeins from the wall of Helvellyn when the foxhounds were 'loosed' on the Rigg one morning this week and went away along the tops towards Thirlmere. One fox, a grey one, sidetracked the hounds somewhere in the crags and they divided, high and low, among the rocks above the Vale of St John's. Just ahead of the lower lot another fox got up, red this time, with a white tail tip, and streaked off through the bracken, jumped to the wall top, turned to look at the excited followers, and climbed towards the little church of St John's-in-the-Vale. It is a very little church which stands nine hundred feet above sea level where, in the thirteenth century, there was a house of the hospitallers of St John. There is a stone-lined spring at the western end reputed to have the coldest water in Cumberland. It is very difficult on some Sunday mornings to pay attention to the service with the great tits swinging among the yewberries outside the rounded windows and the sheep peering cautiously in from the bank outside. There were different sounds this morning – the agitated 'baa' of the disturbed sheep and the music of the hounds, for, as one of the men said, they were 'fair warmin' to it'. It is a good thing that the hounds do not pass on Sundays, too, or it might be even more difficult for some of the congregation to concentrate.

Keswick   14 December, 1951

I met a most unexpected creature last night on the way between the crags and the lake – a pine marten. The last three nights have been nights of brilliant moonlight, for the moon is at the full and its clear light has flooded the valley, touching the snow on the tops, the frost on the ground, and even making the holly leaves sparkle. All the night animals seemed to be taking advantage of the light; the badgers were making a new home on the hill, and although the earth from the previous night's digging was rimed with frost a large new pile of earth marked their activities. The owls were at their hunting as the pine marten hurried across the grass and into the trees at the lakeside. With its distinctive shape and bushy tail it can be mistaken for no other animal.

Thirty years ago they were comparatively common in the screes below the crags. I know they were trapped there in the rocks for their skins, and for the past few years I have seen none. An old huntsman in the Grasmere district used to say that as foxes increased so 'marts' disappeared, for the foxes were their worst enemies. Whether this is true or not I cannot tell, but it is good to think that the marts are back on their old run through the rocks and along by the lake.

Keswick   28 December, 1951

The wind howled last night round the old square chimneys of the farm and every now and then a particularly fierce gust would bring a sweet reek of peat into the kitchen. There, in the lamplight, the snow on the hills and the floods on the roads were all forgotten. The farmer curled and uncurled his stockinged feet before the blaze, his wife knitted on the other side of the hearth, and the old dog slept on the rug. The

twelve days of Christmas have always been kept, up here, as
a holiday as far as possible, and even in these busier times
there is an air of unbuttoned ease about. The 'crack' turned
back through the year with its joys and worries: the fine
autumn and the fell sheep; the horse which, bought specially
for the hay harvest, would only go backwards when put in
the rake; then to the new baby at a nearby farm: 'Aye, they
mun raise it like they do t'hounds, as much fresh milk as it
can sup – and a laal sup ower.' People here take slowly to a
strange face and they once spoke of a newcomer in a
neighbouring town: 'A laal soft beggar as like an Irish cattle
dealer as ivver Ah saw, wi' a gurt red feeace and a laal bow
tie.' I never met, so far as I know, an Irish dealer, but I shall
know what to look for now!

Keswick   *11 January, 1952*

All the windowpanes have gone from the disused mill and
the thick grey cobwebs shivered in a thin wind, the dust on
the floor stirred at the opening of a door and small pieces of
plaster fell from the laths above. The water is running bank-
high below the alders and there is a continual murmur, drip,
and splash as it seeps from the river through the sluice-gates,
finds its way along the stone runway, under the floor, and
down the culvert to the river again. The otters come up the
culvert at dusk, pause in the small outside, and slip up under
the low opening below the wall. A clear, soft whistle, a
splash in the pool, and they are gone, but soon there will be
cubs under the mill and they can be clearly seen through the
holes in the rotting floor. The cold, clear light has not
dimmed enough at four o'clock today for any otters to be
stirring, but it was almost too dim to see the strange jumble
on the windowsill looking out over the river. There was an
old candlestick, its rim long dulled and tarnished; a pair of
stout clogs, worn out in service at the mill; a deer's antler,
brittle with age; and a handful of moths' wings, fawn and
brown and cream. It seemed an odd collection to find
abandoned in an old room disturbed only by wandering
draughts or a hungry mouse.

Keswick
22 February, 1952

I suppose everyone who knows this part of the north has in their minds some particular stretch of country which for them is the essence of the Cumberland scene; for me it is a mountain valley, very high and very lonely, flanked on one side by larch- and juniper-covered hills but rising on the other in two steep pitches of overhanging crag. It is always lonely, but now, with the patches of melting snow on the winter-bleached grass and the glistening sheets and cascades of ice on the rock face, it seems utterly remote and lost. The snow water has swelled the beck which divides the valley, it pours down over the rocks and the small falls throw spray upwards to the bright mosses and ferns which come to the very water's edge; the water itself is dull green and brown with slowly turning wheels of white foam below and beside each fall. The juniper bushes are bent and twisted with many hard winters and brief summers; most are grotesquely shaped but some have a perfect symmetry of glowing green. The sunward sides of the walls are touched by the scarlet pinheads of lichen rising on grey stems. Brought out by the returning warmth a cloud of gnats rises and falls above the wall top; there is no sound except for the rushing waters and the small wind in the rocks.

Keswick
27 November, 1952

The cold north-east wind searches round the corners of the farm buildings, blowing wisps of hay from the byre door across the frozen yard. The geese have gone across the fields to the ice-rimmed pond, the dogs are shut in the stable as they always are if they are not on the fell, and the mistress is busy, so there is quiet under the porch and in the farm kitchen. There is quiet and warmth there but no rest because it is baking day. The fire is stoked up and purrs through the flue at the side of the grate and behind the oven. The glow flickers on the steel fender, along the rather low beams, and reflects on the dresser opposite and on a white apron round a rather ample waist. A warm smell of Grasmere gingerbread fills the air. This is a true traditional recipe which has stood the test of time. Half a pound of butter and half a pound of brown sugar are creamed together with a pinch of salt, some finely chopped candied orange peel, and a tablespoonful of golden syrup. Then one pound of flour is sieved with a dessertspoonful of ginger, a teaspoonful of carbonate of soda, and a teaspoonful of cream of tartar. These are rubbed into the first set of ingredients until all is crumbled and fine and can be pressed lightly with the hand into a shallow tin. More syrup would make the gingerbread softer and is often preferred, but either way it should be baked about an hour in a slow oven and always kept about a month before it is eaten. At Christmas-time it will stand on the dresser beside the mince pies in the friendly glow of lamplight and firelight for anyone who comes to enjoy.

Keswick *19 February, 1953*

Last week the two long gullies on the face of Great End stood out like black gashes up the snowy rocks but now they seem to have sunk back into the rest of the crag and drifts of snow lie only at their feet. Last week the faces of the barren strawberry flowers were splashed with mud and the small advance guard of the celandines had their petals tightly shut, but now both are clean and open to the sun. After a night of steady rain the sun came through the soft February clouds and turned each raindrop on the alders and the birches to white fire. I have not seen the otters for ten days and I waited hopefully at the foot of a long pool this afternoon but still they were not to be seen. Instead a pair of dippers bobbed in and under the river and, screened by the alders, I watched them come to a stump at the water's edge to wash their beaks and sing and dart back to the pool. They struck the top of the water at a low angle and so fast that they appeared to fly under it before they began to swim. Suddenly one bird almost shot to the surface with a small minnow, which looked very large in its beak, struggling wildly. With great vigour the bird slapped it again and again on the water until the silvery thing was limp and quiet. It was eaten on the stump and the fishing began again. As I turned my back on Scafell to come down the river their brief pebble-and-water song consoled me with its beauty for the absence of the otters.

Keswick

11 December, 1953

The valleys and the lower fells are shrouded in mist and this morning, before sunrise, it lay motionless across the moss, leaving only the tops of the birches clear of its white sea. At the top of the crag, where stands a sentinel line of juniper bushes, the world changed completely; the air was clear and the unrisen sun laid a path of light across the sky revealing beside the lichen-bearded stems of the junipers the marks of many deer. Their unseen presence could be sensed and felt, and here, where no human being ever seems to come, is a great ring trodden deep into the turf where the stags have gone round and round in combat. There were jabs in the peat from the antler points, tufts of hair lay on the ground, and in the lowest branches of the larches were rags of peat thrown up from the ground. Just as the sun cleared the fell and struck with dazzling light across the wood, a warning cough sounded from the trees and the creatures began to move away. I did not see them go, but all around me the wood was full of their soft movement and their musky scent. The mist which had risen behind me came swirling up to the edge of the crag, where it met the wind across the fell and was turned over and back in streams of boiling white. Again and again it surged up and was turned back until a cloud covered the sun, the mist and the cloud joined in a damp embrace, and the trees, the rocks, and the deer withdrew into greyness and silence.

Keswick

11 January, 1954

It is perhaps difficult to realise that the Thirlmere Valley with its deep lake, so seldom disturbed except by a very strong wind from the west or the east, is a place where people once lived in comfort or in hardship and loved the land now sunk under the water. Go back a little, however, into the deep fir woods and the old world is still there, hidden and waiting. There are the walls of the fields and the intakes, the ruined barns, and the small round sheepfolds where the sheep, having been collected from the fells, were sorted before they went to their own farms. There too, below one of the highest crags in the valley, is an old 'mart' trap on what was once the accustomed run of the pine martens. It is best to go there in a

147

hard frost because the crag face has weathered very quickly of recent years and chunks of rock are apt to fall from above it in a disconcerting manner. The trap is several yards long made of slabs of stone leant up against the bottom of the crag; the chinks are filled in and the actual traps were set on the path inside the stone tunnel. The martens were numerous a hundred years ago but now they are few, and no man's hand is against them any more, so the slabs are covered with moss and ferns and the whole place has an air of sleeping in the icy quiet; not a bird nor an animal stirred. In the lake there lay reflected the perfect counterpart of Helvellyn, its frozen austerity turned to gold by the declining sun.

Keswick *18 February, 1954*

The other evening an otter floated down below the willows; it flowed with the water rather than swam, and the long chain of bubbles behind it seemed born of the animal and the water. It paused at one of its accustomed fishing places and slid up on to a half-submerged log with barely a ripple. One shake sent the water flying from its outer coat and it froze into immobility, forepaws flexed, and muzzle intent above the stream, until the mass was no longer otter and log but was all otter or all log. There seems to be some deeper affinity between creatures and their surroundings, or the element in which they live, than can be explained by their colouring or their behaviour. They are a part of that element. Yesterday the sun had warmed a strip of sodden, snow-edged turf below a hawthorn hedge and a line of firs, bringing the worms nearer the surface, and, as I approached, a bird dropped on to it and stayed there motionless. I watched equally still until, fearing my eyes had betrayed me and I was watching a block of wood, I moved slightly. In that instant the bird rose up past the hawthorns and the firs; it was a fine woodcock, and its backward glancing eye, so round and full, its long, downward-curving beak, and its spread fan of tail feathers all blended into the green and brown. The block of wood was gone, the spell broken, and from the hedge an aged woodman straightened himself from where he had been stooping, unseen alike by the bird and by me. He too in his mole-coloured clothes belonged in the woods, and I was the only intruder.

Keswick

The sun has risen this morning on a world of cold unearthly beauty. The mountains are covered in shining snow and their magnificence is beyond easy description, but for the fell sheep it may well be tragic unless the thaw comes soon. Yesterday one farmer could only find a few of his sheep and one was already dead, suffocated under the hard surface. Many of them will have found their way to the stone walls which pattern the fell and there, huddled together under deep drifts, they can survive for a long time until they are dug out or the weather changes. On the lower slopes the tracks of the hares and the rabbits showed how far they had travelled in search of food, but the badgers seemed to have been as undaunted by the bitter conditions as they are by most things. The snow had drifted deeply across their setts and only the highest of the holes was sheltered; from it two sets of muddy pawmarks had come and gone and there were many scrapes nearby. The lowest hole had been heavily covered with snow and the big sow badger who lives there had forged up and out with the action of a strong snowplough, leaving a white wave on either side. She had gone to the middle hole and dug her way in through that drift. A clean, warm smell of badger came from all three holes. She must have an excellent sense of the condition of the ground for on her way to the woods in the valley she had skirted the soft drifts and gone boldly over the frozen ones, leaving only sharp claw marks on the hard, glistening surface.

Keswick

There is snow on the mountains and on the tops of the lower fells, so that when the day's work is done and darkness falls the shutters are gladly closed against the night outside. To a visitor the farm kitchen seems a haven of warmth and comfort; the fire burns quietly on the hearth, its light reflected back from the low beams, and the man of the house sits beside it at ease, unbooted and ready to talk or ready to be silent. The women are too busy for much talk at present, for the rug stretcher which has been brought down from the loft is being set up to start a new rag-rug to replace the one by the hearth. The old one is getting rather worn now, but much of it is still bright and all of it is a reminder of the people who made it – anyone may give a hand with a rug. Here is the strip made by Molly the night she fell off her ancient bicycle as she went home down the valley and damaged it but not herself; here is the corner shaded like autumn leaves which was done by the girl with nimble fingers; and here is rather an untidy bit made by one who is usually referred to as being 'rather a clarty body'. The rags lie in a basket beside the stretcher and the prodders on top of them, and each of these has its own history. One is a bright steel pin so old that no one remembers its first owner; another is a tine of a deer's horn, its first shedding, found in the woods; and the third is of golden boxwood polished smooth with age.

Keswick   24 December, 1954

A dark day at the year's end is a good time to look through the hoard of feathers I have collected on my wanderings, and remember the past year. Among them are the pathetic bright crest of a goldfinch killed by a hawk in the plantation; blue jay's feathers, the common currency of the woods; a barred feather fallen from a buzzard's tail; and the widely varying browns of snipe, grouse, and woodcock. These last I have only recently got after the migrant woodcock came in their dozens to a stand of old oak above the Solway one night of full moon in November. Those I favour perhaps most belong to the ducks: the shimmering blue of a mallard's wing feather; small red-brown feathers from a pochard's neck; speckled widgeon feathers and a prized copper-green feather from a pintail drake. I recall, too, the places where I found them, and particularly the marshes on a bitter day when, stooping low over the skeleton of a mallard in the tussocky grass, I heard the beat of heavy wings and saw eleven whooper swans coming low over my head to the water, unmindful of my presence. As they saw me they towered up on the icy wind with a great beating of wings and an indignant barking, and rose in a massy clump of white.

At the very bottom of the box is a small tuft of grey, characteristically crinkled, badger's hair that I found caught on a low fence beside the sett. I keep it for its association and not, I hope, because 'a tuft of hair gotten from the head of a full-grown brock is powerful to ward off all manner of witchcraft.'

Keswick   *18 February, 1955*

Last May disaster overtook my favourite colony of badgers: they were gassed, although in all the years I knew them they never did any harm in the countryside. During this winter their deserted setts have given cover to a number of foxes – much less desirable tenants than the badgers – but I think one or two of the badgers must have escaped for a new home is being set up elsewhere. I have not seen the occupants yet. I went there this morning as the snow was beginning to fall after a night of crackling frost and brilliant stars and found that it had been a night of hard work for the badgers. One of the holes, previously tenanted by a rabbit, had been much enlarged; a pile of fresh earth lay at its mouth, a thick root had been bitten through and pulled aside, and the snow was patterned with large, muddy pawmarks. There were scrapes on an old tree where powerful claws had been sharpened. The new home has much in its favour: there is a spinney to protect it from the cold winds; shaly earth which is good for badgers' earthworks and for a watcher's background; a spring at the wood's edge and, perhaps best of all, a kindly farmer. As I stood there an icy wind sighed in the spinney and snow sifted on to the badger's path, but a thrush foretold spring, undaunted, from an oak and I wondered if a new home meant a young badger family, for as the thrush kept saying over and over, the time is right, the time is right.

Keswick   *5 January, 1956*

So often in early January there seems to be a pause in winter – a time to draw breath; there was frost and snow in December and probably there is worse to come, but now, at least, the valleys and mountains are calm and still. The skies are laden with cloud and mist, which may disappear later in the day, but which are slow to clear in the early mornings. This morning the mist is doing odd things to the shapes of the mountains: it lies in a dense cloud over the cold waters of Lodore Falls, whose voice is loud with recent rain. It is rising in long streaks up the face of Great End and Scafell and is caught in wisps on the lesser mountains – High Scawdel, Glaramara, and Grange Fell – whose names are like a necklace round the Vale of Borrowdale. But close at hand there are other smaller and more vivid beauties – the shining green of water-fed mosses, grey lichen with scarlet points, and the long green fronds of ferns unspoiled, as yet, by winter.

By the plumed reeds of the lake an otter is fishing methodically, rising at long intervals to snort the water from its nostrils or, it would almost seem, to pause for reflection. It is too far away to see clearly, but I count myself fortunate to see an otter at all in broad daylight and I think the sight of its flowing grace as it rolls up and back again into the water a full reward for a cold wait, a crick in the neck, and a pair of cold, wet feet.

Keswick   29 March, 1956

It is two years since the badgers were gassed in the big sett on the fell, and although it was visited at times by roving badgers it was not properly occupied until this winter. Last night the late blackbirds scolded the first brown owls; a curlew cried, melancholy, from the marsh. A grouse flew across the fell outlined against the green northern sky and it, too, scolded before it settled for the night. A hare came leisurely downhill, passed within six feet of me, and stopped on the badgers' pile of earth to sniff and listen. Earlier in the year the sett mouth was stopped with bracken, a sure sign that there were young cubs below, and now, as further evidence, there are very frequent changes of bedding. When the light was almost gone a rush of badger scent and a scrabble of claws showed that the sow was at the entrance to the sett, and when she emerged her behaviour and aspect proved the presence of cubs. She was intent, concentrated, and almost furtively quiet in her movements; she came uphill collecting small heaps of dry bracken and lastly a smaller pile of dead grass, and then – with a most characteristic badger movement – she paused and backed, gathering each pile with a scythe sweep of her forelegs and hitching them under her belly, and slid, sledge-like, downhill and into the sett. Her day's work had begun.

Keswick

Sometimes you come across in a quiet fold of the northern hills a person whose aspect, indeed, whose whole attitude to things about him, is a living proof of some proud, forgotten ancestry. In one such place there is an elderly woman whose head with its high cheekbones, tall forehead, and noble carriage would not look out of place on an old coin and whose tongue is as keen as her mind. She was talking about 't'rough ground near Cunningarth', where she had lived as a child and where now a number of archaeologists are laying bare the three occupations, one above the other, of the Romano-British settlement which lies outside the Roman fort, Olenacum, at 'Old Carlisle'. To me, an inexpert helper, the finding of the broken pots and the everyday things of those occupations is an exciting task. It seems a pleasant place, too, this green plateau between Skiddaw and Solway where the skylarks sing in the blue November air as happily as they probably did over the smoking ruins of the first town or the walls of its successors. But to the woman in the hills it is otherwise; she is still repelled and fascinated by something she is part of and does not understand. 'Maybe it was t'travellers (gipsies) who camped down by t'beck an' maybe not; I feared to go by t'place at dusk when I was sent on errands – there was more there than you'd ever see.' Go there at night and you might agree with her. The sleeping countryside has a power all its own.

Keswick

The dark alleyways which lead back from the marketplace are not used as they once were; many are fallen into decay. But one at least of the men who worked there long ago remembers the ups and downs of his apprenticeship. He made tallow candles and it was not a job for the squeamish; indeed tallow-boiling was only allowed at night, so much did it offend the other citizens' noses. 'Aye,' he says, 'much of t'stuff you see in t'meat shops would have been candles in them days. We collected t'fat from t'butchers an' t'farmers until we had a copper full – an' you knew about it in t'summertime. I'd finish mi job in t'shop – seventy-two hours I worked some weeks for twelve and sixpence – hev mi tea an' a bit of a play an' be back before ten o'clock to start heating t'fat.' As it heated, the rubbish – grubs too, sometimes – was skimmed from the surface with a big ladle and when the fat was clear the sticks were lowered in. There were twenty-four wicks on a cane, six canes to a rack, all dipped once and allowed to dry – a slow process in summer – and dipped again until the required thickness was achieved. There were either eighteen or twelve candles to a pound, costing fourpence ha'penny a pound, and they went for farmers' lanterns or to the lead and barytes mines near here or at Ullswater, or the slate quarries in Borrowdale. It is not difficult to imagine the quarrymen at the mouth of the now disused slate quarry at Bowderstone picking up fistfuls of clay for candlesticks and disappearing, tallow candle in hand, into the green, damp gloom.

Keswick   30 November, 1956

In future no more barns are to be built in the traditional pattern which has prevailed in the Lake District for so long and which, I am told, has a parallel only in the Scandinavian countries. They are large stone buildings with byres and calfpens below and storage space above. Usually a ramp of stone and earth leads to the upper floor, so that a hay cart can be driven up and into the haymew to unload, and in the winter the hay is thrown down or carried down a fodder-gang to the cows below. The byres are often dark, and there is in many of them little free passage for air, but they are cool in summer and warm in winter; indeed, potatoes are stored above the cows' warmth to preserve them from frost. The barns shelter a number of strange, clean little rooms where objects have collected like driftwood, and unused harness jostles with yearly-used shearing benches, meal chests, and hay-timing gear. These places vary greatly in age, but in a recent one, built in 1855, the beam above the haymew door is of one solid oak trunk and on the walls at either side hang thick fringes of green fern. The door is more often open than shut; in summer swifts fly screaming through it and out at the window opposite, which frames a picture of the distant fells. Owls always haunt the place and in winter bats and butterflies dream away the bitter months among the rafters in a maze of cobwebs and bits of hay. Modern barns have no place for them.

154

Keswick

There are some animals so rare and shy that few people ever
see them and indeed it is often pure luck that eventually
brings a glimpse of them. Pine martens are such creatures. I
saw them here in the days when they were more plentiful
than they are now, and I saw one again in December 1951,
but lately my only rewards have been a line of pawmarks, or
even one solitary pawmark on a muddy path below some
crags or deep in a fir wood. Sometimes there are droppings
on the ledges of the crags or other small signs. Two years ago
one was seen in full daylight on a stone ledge above one of
the lakes, and now not far from that place a series of puzzling
happenings are being attributed – rightly or wrongly – to a
pine marten.

The hens at the farm are shut up in a barn at night, some
fields and a beck away from the main buildings, and one
morning recently three were found dead and partly eaten
inside their barn. The hens went in through a trap door
which closed behind and left no egress except for a creature
much smaller and more 'lish' than a hen. So the hunt was
fetched and a very small fox was caught – 't'laal varmint' was
gone and all would be well – but next morning a large
number of hens were dead and the rest terrified. No decent-
sized fox, otter, or badger could have got at the hens, and
local opinion is adamant: it must be a 'mart'.

Keswick

There is no doubt that Champ, the foxhound, is, in his
middle years, one of the most useful of the Blencathra pack.
What he has lost in speed he has gained in wisdom; he has
never foolishly run hares, deer, or any other creatures and his
sole interest is foxes. Yet that does not wholly sum up his
interest – like any other hound his belly is inclined to be his
god and so today with the snow hard frozen on the fells, the
hunting poor, and the foxes secure in a white, scentless
world, he has come home to the farm where he spends his
summers. His smiling face appears at dinnertime at the
kitchen window, his lip raised in a grin of, 'Here I am and
where's the food?' He will go back in his own good time,
probably leaving at the weekend to be at the kennels on

Blencathra side to greet the home-coming pack, the huntsman, and the whip after their week away. The huntsman does not really resent Champ's temporary desertion; he appreciates his seven winters' service, his offspring who already run with the pack, and his usual steadiness. Indeed the huntsman's words one day lately to the dogs as they checked on a confused scent and Champ's urgent voice rallied the rest sums it all up best: 'Hark,' he said, 'hark an' listen to Champ, you silly beggars, hark an' ga 'til 'im.'

Keswick   16 January, 1958

The disused mill stands beside the weir on an elbow of land thrust out into the river and across the water rises an ivy-matted cliff of rock. The river is in flood and all the thunderous noise of the weir is trapped between the cliff and the mill, whose ancient walls quiver and vibrate with sound. It is a long time since the mill was used, its pale sandstone lintels – so lovingly made – have sunk a little on their stone pillars; the stone steps to the empty upper rooms have canted slightly to one side and are slippery with moss. Spleenwort and hart's-tongue dip long green fingers into the spray of the river and into the quieter runnel of the millrace where it slips through the rotting sluice-gate and under the mill floors.

   The otters used to rear their cubs under the broken floors but old Tom says they have been gone for two years now. No, he says, no one has harmed them, who would want to harm such gentle creatures who eat so many eels? No, they have just changed their ways as otters do. Perhaps old Tom does not see everything which goes on after dark, and though the otters may not have their nursery there now they have not forgotten their secret road up from the river below, along the choked mill-lade and into the stone maze below the walls where the sound of the weir is almost stilled. A line of otter pawmarks in the mud has its own tale to tell.

Keswick   5 December, 1958

The badgers are making drastic alterations to their home on the fell, two new levels have been driven in, one at the side of the present holes and another below the huge pile of earth which they have excavated during numbers of years. I went to see the progress yesterday evening just after the sunset. It was very cold and clear; a party of redwings whistled in the hawthorn hedges and the badgers' newest hole looked as if a small engine had been at work the previous night backing out, leaving a deep groove and a pile of earth and stones at its outer end. I walked very carefully round it and left a fresh slice of honeycomb on a foxglove leaf beside the upper hole. I have no wish to tame the badgers, even if it was possible, or even to make them less distrustful of human beings but, in the past, I have left similar presents and even watched the badgers enjoy them and look hungrily for more. I went back this morning while the white hoar-frost was still stuck on the ground and ribbons of scarlet cloud hung in the eastern sky. It was obvious that more hard work had been done: there were badger footmarks everywhere and the hoar-frost was gone from all the holes except one – the one where the honey still lay on the foxglove leaf. I must, somehow, have tainted it with my hands and it may be days before that hole is used again.

Keswick
27 February, 1959

When counting the signs of spring, however reluctant, it is quite impossible to overlook the extreme bad temper of many of the garden birds. Not for them, as yet, is the mild sweetness of song but rather fury and cries of defiance. Two thrushes have just joined battle in the hedge having chased one another wildly in and out of the trees and across the garden; the chaffinches, blue tits, and blackbirds, provide minor explosions and only the dunnocks, unobtrusive as usual, preserve their calm. The human population is not exempt from its troubles, mostly due to colds of varying malignity and their after-effects – and in this part of the world there is a nice distinction in the degrees of being 'poorly' which covers everything from slight indisposition to serious illness. One starts by being 'poorly' or 'not so good' and worsens to 'middlin''. Indeed, a farmer who recently nearly lost his life in an encounter with a bull confessed to being 'nobbut middlin'' for two or three days. It is only a short step between 'nobbut middlin'' and shaken heads and silence. However, once the sufferer begins to recover he is said to be 'ga'in on', and even if the illness has 'fair tekken t'fleece off him' (and who, having seen a sheep losing its coat, can doubt the aptness of the simile?) he will at last be 'ga'in on gaily' or 'gaily weel'. One son said of his sire, 'There's nowt wrong wi' Fadder, he's nobbut a bit shakked at knees,' and the old man himself might even have replied, as another who was known the length of the vale invariably did when asked, 'Ah'm beautiful'.

Keswick   *6 November, 1959*

Had anyone been walking one cold, sunny afternoon lately through the fields near the foot of Skiddaw they would have met an odd procession – two people carrying a ladder and a third with a bulging sack and two hats draped in black net. One of the old oaks here cast a huge branch on a windless day about a month ago exposing a raw, jagged hole where a swarm of honey bees have lived for five years. I had only heard of them at midday and this was an attempt to shelter them before the frost came. The bees seemed docile enough from below but as soon as the ladder went up they were out and looking for trouble. On a second trip up the ladder a cloud from a bee-smoker drove most of them deep into the oak and left empty the lovely complex of their combs.

Some of the combs were old, dark stuff, some this year's pale, honey-filled wax, and since it seemed impossible to remove the bees we decided to nail a sack over the hole. This was not an easy task at the top of a ladder in a crowd of interested bees even with a bee-hat and a smoker as protection, but it was done. Two of us tied an old plastic macintosh, by its arms, round the tree and nailed its body over the sack. It certainly looks a bit eerie in the dusk, but now the bees – who dread damp more than cold – have a chance, with their stored honey, to survive to see the spring. Who knows? I may take that swarm next May.

Keswick   *3 December, 1959*

Hospitality has always been part of the north, where it springs almost wholly from goodness of heart and owes only a very little to the interest a visitor can bring to a lonely hill farm. I went yesterday unheralded and with nothing to offer to a farm on the slope of Skiddaw. Dusk was thickening and the white ducks half-asleep outside the kitchen door glimmered, more than life-size, and lights shone dimly in the byre. The sons of the farm were already milking but the daughters, on their way to their outside tasks, and the father and mother now almost retired from work, were having a last mug of tea. The oil-lamp was lit in the kitchen and though it left mysterious shadows in the rafters, where bunches of dried herbs and two hams hung just above head height, it glowed on a clutter of farm tackle on the dresser and on the pictures of farm horses on the walls. Almost by magic, it seemed, there was a white cloth on the scrubbed table, and there was homemade bread and tea-cakes thickly spread with farm butter. There were jam and plum cake, shortbread, and cherry cake, and a huge apple plate-cake – all homemade too. The tea was hot and sweet – all part of a warm little world shut in from the dark outside.

And what did we talk about? We talked of our children, the absent ones, of parish affairs, of the sleepy adders curled for winter in the peat stacks, and of the boldness of the foxes who bark at nights on the fell and try a staring-match with the farmer in daylight. I had gone to the farm to buy eggs but who in such a situation could mix business with pleasure?

Keswick

It all began over Champ the foxhound; he is in his tenth winter with the local pack and evidently feels that the time has come for him to pick his hunting days and so, finding himself one day lately near the farm where he spends his summers, he left the other dogs to carry on and dropped in to see what there was to eat. There was a tremendous buffet at the door and in he came 'laughing his head off', as the farmer's wife said. He really does laugh, lifting his lip up off his teeth, shaking his head to one side with joy, and giving everyone the full benefit of his pleasure. 'Daft as a swill', she called him and that did it – how daft can one be? There are many variants – 'daft as a yat' (gate), 'daft as a brush', and 'daft as a wagon-horse'. At first it is difficult to see any connection between them all, but it is very simple, really. 'Owt is daft 'at does all t' hard work', was the general opinion. 'What carries all t' heavy loads? T' swill. T' yat's for

159

ivver being opened an' shut an' if you want to deu owt in t'yard t'brush gets all t'mucky jobs. An' as for t'wagon-horse – think of all t'rivin' an'pullin' an'sniggin' (clearing small timber) it does – it mun be daft t' deu all that.' There are, however, degrees of daftness and the farmer had the last word who said: 'All t' nicest fowk are a laal bit daft any road.'

Keswick   1 December, 1960

This district, as one might expect, abounds in fox stories, many of them astonishing and a lot of them true unless, of course, they happen to be told by one of the local wags, who also abound. The general opinion of a fox's intelligence is not very high, but some of them have character, like the one who chased two working terriers and later a sheepdog down the breast of Skiddaw and the tame one who let its owner's dogs hunt it under Blencathra on Sunday afternoons. One dewy morning lately a farmer heard a sharp yapping coming from behind a wall below Helvellyn and thinking there must also be cubs and waiting to see what emerged was astonished to see a large black cat leap to the wall top closely followed by a fox. There they faced each other, the cat bristling in every hair, the fox yapping and making feints – no doubt hoping that the cat would turn and run, making itself more vulnerable. At last it did so, but it travelled so fast that it gained the next wall top after a tremendous sprint. This time the fox stayed below still yapping and then, for no visible reason, suddenly turned back to the fell. The farmer was convinced that the cat was his old Jet, but there were no wet pawmarks on the kitchen step and Jet sat by the range 'as dry as snuff'. Foxes certainly stick faithfully to their paths. I used to smell them in my garden in the early morning long after this house was built, and quite near to it, on what was once their lonely hilltop path.

Keswick   11 January, 1961

The hollow ash tree, out on the edge of the lake-marsh, which has cradled so many generations of white owls, has fallen at last. It creaked its way through the midsummer rains while the latest of the owl families was fledging, groaned and

complained in the autumn winds, and finally succumbed to a
winter gale. Its frailty is now very apparent: the trunk was
simply a hollow shell crowned by a ring of growing branches
and its inside was filled with layers of decayed wood, soil,
fungus, owl pellets, and all their leavings. These are now
strewed on the grass. There is a confusion of small, white,
lace-like bones of mice, voles and shrews with many skulls
intact showing characteristic orange-coloured teeth. There
are the bigger bones of rats and other creatures, a bird skull
or two, and a fine selection of the elytra of beetles. These
vary from the big black cases of ground beetles and brownish
cases of cockchafers to the little iridescent ones of the smaller
beetles, shining blue and green among the general mass. The
owls were not to be found in any of their usual places this
morning: the ivied ash by the water whose roots sometimes
give shelter to the otters was deserted, so was the shattered
willow and the very tall, old ash where owl pellets run out
like a stream at the bottom of the trunk. They must, I think,
be living up to their other name and have taken to a barn for
the winter, and who could blame them?

Keswick 10 *March,* 1961

This is Champ the foxhound's eleventh winter with the
Blencathra foot-pack, eleven winters of hard going on some
of the most mountainous country anywhere on which
hounds run. He is slower now, of course, and is father and
grandfather of some of the pack; they show their family
likeness in their big frames and their wisdom – and in other
ways, too. He brought one of his sons recently, when the
hunt was in the neighbourhood, to visit the farm where he
spends his summers. He is well fed there but also makes his
rounds of the tents which dot the valley and he never
overlooks a stray hen's nest. Both dogs hunted about the
place, scavenging everywhere, until they spotted a hen nicely
settled on the top of the sett-pot outside the old cottage
across the yard. 'Them dogs,' said the farmer's wife, 'ull beat
us to that egg,' and so they did. It was gulped down, warm,
from below the hen. Champ usually visits the sett-pot and if
no hen is sitting, jumps up and crams all of himself, except
his massive rear, through the small window behind it just to
see if any meat-meal has been left about. Lately he followed

two ladies, doubtless with sandwiches in their pockets, through a farm down the valley where the farmer – knowing Champ – caught him and shut him up. He was released later and went gaily home, but was back next day to clear out a hen's nest overlooked in the barn; eggs, foxes, or campers' bacon, all are of interest to Champ.

Keswick   *16 November, 1961*

Pet lambs are often a mixed blessing. The pet lamb at the farm, in size more sheep than lamb, was supposed to be in the quarry this morning at the back of the house, but in truth she was below the kitchen window. She stood there, black-faced and independent, indeed defiant, chewing the cud with a long green bramble trailing from her rear. Had she been human, one would have said she was eavesdropping. Had that been so she would certainly have heard no good of herself, 'A bad, black-faced laal beggar', was only one of the terms used of her. Back in the spring when she was very young she was the joy of all visitors, especially those with cameras, and certainly she made a charming picture taking her bottle greedily from the hands of the small blonde granddaughter of the farm. Indeed, food has never ceased to be her first interest and it has nearly proved her undoing several times. Nothing comes amiss: she waits round the corner of the house, peeping at times to see if the back door is open and unattended so that she may slip in and sample the dog food, pig food, or even hen 'crowdie', and only last week she jumped into a bucket of milk in the byre. Once she got the calves' food and ate until she was in agony; indeed, everyone thought she would die – as she might have done if the farmer's wife had not poured a whole bottle of the baby's dill water down her gullet.

Keswick   *10 January, 1962*

Until a few days ago there was a layer of ice under the wet grass in the garden; now it is gone and although there is snow on the fells a few frost-bitten daisies open each morning on the lawn and the winter gnats dance in the cold air. It is only later, when the new green should be springing in the garden, that the full toll of the frost will show. It has been a wonderful midwinter for the ravens and there is plenty of carrion for them on the fell-top, to judge by their numbers and their – for them – cheerful croakings. The hive bees have come through well so far, but one hive is decidedly bad-tempered. The mice found their way into it from the field outside, chewed up the bees' covering, and – what must have really upset the colony – made their way up through the frames of half-sleeping bees to steal their stores.

I think we change creatures' habits more than we realise by giving them food; the number of birds in gardens, half-dependent on scraps, is obvious to most people but, to me, some of the red squirrels seem to have changed even more. I was brought up in a house beside sprawling woodlands where the squirrels slept away most of the winter, disappearing for long stretches and reappearing, thin and hungry, in the spring. A friend of mine who feeds red squirrels regularly and well tells me that even in the bitterest weather hers have never ceased to come, sometimes five at a time. Or is it, partly, too, that the recent milder winters have made the squirrels less inclined to sleep?

Keswick   10 January, 1963

There is no doubt that the otters enjoy snow and ice. It is possible to find slides they have used in play on the river-banks where the slope is steep enough to take them down-bank towards the water, but I have never seen them in action. My young cat treats the snow in much the same way and is otter-like in looks – short, sleek coat and over-long tail. He has a variety of snow games. He follows a thrown snowball, which skims the surface of the frozen lawn, at a fast gallop which often ends in a four-pawed skid or on his side sweeping the ice clear of its snow-covering.

The otters have snug homes in the river-bank and the cat his fireside but the hares who live on these upland meadows can find little comfort in this bitter weather. I met one last night near midnight in the moonlight and deep snow near the Castle Rigg stone circle. It was searching for food and it looked thin and seemed much slower than hares usually do until it found an opening in the wall where a beck runs out of the field and then it was off over the hill. It looked very big and dark, however, against the moon-shining snow and its shadow ran with it as it went. The ground inside and round the stone circle is criss-crossed with hare tracks and the moonlight showed, too, where the snow was plastered against the stones and cast long blue shadows on the hard ground. It touched the flanks of the encircling hills – Saddleback, Helvellyn, and the Derwentwater fells and, far to the east, the long line of the Pennines, as substantial as a silver cloud.

Keswick   *7 February, 1963*

The lake since it froze seems to have completely changed its character – who would have thought that small and friendly Derwentwater could be so arctic? One day earlier this week it seemed to have grown in size and out towards its centre one was surrounded by a glitter almost painful to the eyes, for the ice was covered with dry, powdery snow made up of millions of ice-crystals shining and flashing in the early morning sun. Mallards were gathered in a patch of open water where a stream runs in and a few ducks slept, breast-down, on the far ice, but otherwise there was not a soul about and, for the most part, all was silent. Blue shadows which looked like open water were cast by the trees on the islands but Rampsholm, one of the smaller islands, only added to its illusion of a desolate, arctic landscape. Cormorants have perched and roosted for years now on its ageing pines; their droppings whitewash trunks and branches, and now some of the trees are dead, thrusting up bone-pale, bone-clean fingers to the sky. The smell is appalling and on one of the fingers rested a solitary cormorant, black against the white. How different was St Herbert's hermit-island: most of its trees thrive and the sycamore buds are green and swelling. The rooks, encouraged by the sun, quarrelled happily over their nests, even stealing a few sticks from one another to stake out a claim on the spring which seems so far ahead. Today everything is blotted out in a heavier fall of snow.

Keswick

It is interesting to see how well the red squirrels have
weathered this hard winter. They have slept less than one
would expect and I have met them throughout even the
coldest spells and in all sorts of places but especially in the
sheltered woods near the lakes and on sunny fellsides. The
mixed woodlands – conifers (including yews), beeches, oaks,
cherries, and hazels – all have food to offer and sometimes the
ground under the trees is littered with their leavings. Red
squirrels are fed at a number of houses in this district all the
year round and this, I think, is creating a change in squirrel
status. They seem brisk and well and their greyish winter
coats, which look almost as if they were dusted with frost,
are sleek and shining. They come occasionally to my garden,
especially in autumn, to steal honeycomb put out for the bees
to clean, but one day lately a fat squirrel was enjoying the tits'
coconut on a birch outside the windows much to the fury of
the tits and the avid interest of my young cat who, born and
bred on the Mendips, has probably never seen a red squirrel
before. He crouched, breathless with excitement, on the sill
and was delighted to chase the squirrel straight up the birch,
which became a flurry of wild cat, agitated squirrel, and
angry tits. He came obediently to a whistle but it was some
time before the squirrel was calm enough to descend, and it
will, I think, be even longer before it returns. It is sad that
squirrels are another hazard, in spring, for the woodland-
nesting birds – already so hard hit.

Keswick

'Nice, bonny fresh green hay' – could any words be more
evocative of summer and green fields? These seem strange
words to use of last summer's crop in a year which most
people will remember for its wetness, but they are quite
logical. The question of silage had come up as the evening
wore on round the farm hearth; silage is stuff which can smell
pleasantly yet which, made in wet weather, can do the exact
opposite but, either way, the cows love it. At present on this
hill farm they are having the 'green hay' from 1963 and every
armful you carry, the farmer says, 'Smells lovely and never a
stalk wasted.' It is, he adds, the best hay they have ever had in

all the years he has farmed here and it was all got in the ten days following 25 July. One year when the crop was still being led with horses and carts, the carts were littered with broken, useless hay after each load. Idly the talk turned from horses and carts to tractors and to the small grandson of the farm whose heart, at present, is given to tractors. He will probably be a farmer too, and his grandmother says he already has a 'back like a farmer', echoing a phrase once in common use here. It began with a hawker who went round with a basket on his bicycle crying his fresh herrings – 'A shilling a dozen, backs like farmers, bellies like bank managers.' Some things change; some do not.

Keswick   8 March, 1965

There have been few cloudless mornings lately but the sun rose in a clear sky this snowy March morning and laid a glitter of light along the ridge of Helvellyn until one mountain-top after another caught the brightness. The snow looks deceptively smooth and how deceptive this smoothness is is well shown in the deep lane which leads to Castle Rigg stone circle along the highland dividing this valley from the next. Here the blizzard has created a world of its own, unlike any other. The snow is often hedge or wall height but in gateways it has been swept clear of the ground and curves away in a long drift, breaking like a frozen wave at its crest. It has blown over and even through the dry-stone walls leaving snow bosses and buttresses and repeating the pattern of waves in innumerable differing shapes.

The sun has not yet melted the stars and crystals at their edges and the going is hard – waist-deep in places. Only one set of footprints precede mine but if humans cannot use the lane other creatures can – and do. Many rabbits have been here, a hare in a hurry, and several foxes who have run on the frozen snow cornices and the wall tops. At one gate corner a pungent reek of fox lies on the air in spite of the cold.

The stone circle comes into its own in the snow – remote, unvisited. Some of its stones are plastered with weird, uncertain snow-patterns, and most of them have, in their lee, a patch of bare ground and then a long, twisting hog's back of snow and a line of blue shadow broken by frost-starred stems of last year's grasses.

Keswick

There is often a wind out on the lake-marshes even when the
rest of the valley is comparatively still, and so it was the other
morning, for although the sun was warm for November, a
cold easterly air stirred the bleached sedges and sent long
ripples down the river and out across the lake. The river is
still full but it is clear now, brown and gold leaves float down
it, twisting as they go, and, far down, one can see thick green
waterweed also swaying with the current. A surprised
golden-eye drake, whose green head and white face-patch
flashed in the sunlight, took off from under the willows,
disturbing everything near at hand. The noise of his going,
however, did not disturb three whooper swans, the first
heralds of real winter, who were fast asleep in a reedy inlet.
Their long necks were laid down, their heads under their
wings, and they seemed too tired after their long journey
from the north to be bothered with anything until a pack of
widgeon rose from almost beside them. That brought the
heads up – yellow beaks notched with black – and I felt an
intruder, a disturber of the peace, and left as quickly as I
could.

There was no sign of otters by the water, only a line of
pad-marks on a short cut to the river, but the badgers, by
contrast, had been very busy overnight in the oak wood
above the path. Molehills were overturned, moss and turf
uprooted. I looked back from the trees and saw the swans
still bobbing gently on their pool, heads down again and
peacefully asleep.

Keswick

Any bridge or river-crossing has a fascination; many of them
have been built, or rebuilt, on the same site for centuries and
they must always have been a focus of life, and, for me, few
places have greater fascination than the stone pack-horse
bridges of this district. It was comparatively late in historical
time that people here – traders and travellers alike – got
bridges wide enough to take wheeled traffic and much of the
abuse heaped on the old roads was due to the fact that a
pack-horse train needed so little – for them a roughish track
and a narrow, humpbacked bridge with a steep rise and fall

sufficed. There are few of these bridges left now, but one of them, Smethwaite Bridge, is at Thirlmere, upstream of the new main road and near a farm named, appropriately, Bridge End. Of this bridge only the centre span remains, with wooden planks at either end, but what is left – lichened and ferned – looks strong enough to last a few more centuries. Life has almost left it now but mallard and moorhens haunt the water; watercress and bitter cress grow green near its feet and today a cold wind soughed in the reeds. There is no growth in the willow buds, which is just as well, because there is old snow under the field-crests and probably more to come. This is a broader bridge than most pack-horse bridges and, indeed, it is possible that Daniel Heckstetter, who brought his family from Augsburg over Dunmail Raise in 1572 in a carriage with a tilt over it, to manage the royal mines at Keswick, could have come this way. It is said that the early stone bridges here were built by stone-masons thrown out of work by the dissolution of the monasteries – if that is so they have worn well.

Keswick

It is almost impossible at this time of the year to count heads in the badger population. Feet are much simpler and a February snowfall is a blessing for this. Badgers' times are erratic in winter; they do not hibernate, but there is a tendency to lie in and not to rise with the brown owls as badgers often do and, anyhow, the cold at night would check even the most ardent badger-watcher. It is usually quite easy to say who – badger, fox or rabbit – is using a hole, their ways are so different. But occasionally there is doubt, especially where a number of holes are near together. So one morning lately, before anyone else was about, I visited various holes in a radius of a few miles. Some were strongholds from which the badgers were driven years ago and are trying to re-colonise, some are wholly new and some have never known disturbance in over fifteen years. The snow was very useful; it recorded all pawmarks (proving a fox's tenancy of one hole), it showed where the badgers had gone during the night, what they had dug for (mostly bluebell bulbs in one place) and even what their timing was.

Snow had drifted over one hole in the night, seemingly between the badger's going out and coming in because there was only an inward line of prints and the drift was flattened by a very muddy undercarriage. The wind was thin on the fell but there was still a scent of badger, the mud was unfrozen round some holes and dried grass had been dragged in. There will be cubs soon but it will be a long time before they, or I, are out on the fell in the dusk.

Flookburgh *6 February, 1967*

What do you see in your mind's eye if you think of 'silver' – clouds after rain, light striking a wave's edge or the sparkle of dew in sunlight? Perhaps it is none of these things – for me, now, silver will always recall a mass of newly caught whitebait as I saw them recently in the yard of a fisherman's house on the Lancashire sands. These tiny fishes shine and glitter and glint like a living stream of silver. They are still much esteemed by epicures as they once were in London when whitebait suppers (caught at Blackwall) were the thing, and though whitebait have gone now from polluted rivers they thrive here in cleaner, quieter waters. They are caught in seine nets with a one-and-a-half-inch mesh and with them last week were a small number of smelts, a much more unusual catch and one I had never seen before. The fishermen here call them 'sparling'. They are middle-depth swimmers and are silver, too, a bright almost transparent silver with a hint of green, quite small and very slender with big mouths and an adipose fin (the mark of the salmon family), but their real peculiarity is their smell – the fresh, clean smell of a newly cut cucumber. My older cookery books say they are much esteemed and one (of 1823) speaks especially highly of them, but they are no longer sought for on this coast, although this fisherman's forebears were set up to get them. Indeed, he says both his dad and his grandad (and he is not a young man) knew them well and could smell sparling among the other fish in their nets at three hundred yards on a clear, still night. That is not, I am sure, a fisherman's story; these men of the sands knew – know – their job.

Keswick   8 January, 1968

The first week of the new year often brings strange weather as if it is undecided as to which season it belongs to and one milder morning lately, with soft clouds resting on the snowy fells, there was a smell of growing things in the air. It was an indefinable smell – not the flowering witch hazel, the swelling daphne, or even the balsam poplar whose buds, though furled, can send out sweetness. It was, rather, the exhalation of the earth itself and a promise of growth to come. There were a few wintry daisies in the grass but they are as scentless as snow. At one time foxes used this garden as a pathway (after all it was there before the garden came) and they often left a rank scent on the air but now they come no more and I must go farther afield to meet them. I saw a fine, bracken-red fox early one morning last week as I went up the road to the small church of St John, on the ridge between St John's Vale and the Naddle Valley. It was completely absorbed in its own affairs and very cat-like in its stance (a fox is not really a 'dog' to me), it stood motionless, its brush perfectly erect, only quivering slightly at the tip, and its sharp nose pointed at a tuft of winter-pale grass. Then, with no warning at all it pounced, paws landing with a 'bang' in the tuft – and another vole had had its day. Only then did the fox acknowledge other presences, and even when the farmer with whom I stood pointed his stick – gun-like – it only moved off leisurely and even paused on the skyline to look back before fading, red, into the red bracken.

Keswick   20 January, 1969

Does it surprise anyone that there is only one working horse now living between the Westmorland border of Dunmail Raise and Keswick – and that one, Sandy, works in the

Thirlmere forests on 'banks' too steep for tractors? It surprises me. Horses in Cumberland were numerous in proportion to other livestock in the Middle Ages, for tenants were required to keep horses capable of carrying a man (often in armour) to fight the Scots and therefore horses were used on the land here rather than oxen. Some of the farm horses were characters as well as their masters – like the horse who always brought his sleeping master safely home from market. It had, however, learnt to stop at all the pubs on the way, much to the chagrin of its other users. Sandy, too, is one of a long succession – Old Tib (who could turn a cart in its own length), Bob and Royal, and Charlie and Billy – but life was hard in the steep woods and on the hilly roads and one should not regret their passing but, rather, pause to read the small stone in the wall on Dunmail Raise. It is dated 1843 and reads: 'Fallen from his fellows' side the steed below is lying, in harness here he died – his only fault was dying.'

Keswick   *23 November, 1970*

I often wonder if it is realised what changes have taken place in this district over the years? I do not mean new roads, forests, or even water schemes but smaller, less obvious, and no less important ones. Take the head of Derwentwater and its eastern shore as an example – the growth on the marshes at the lake's head was not always as coarse as it is now. Globe flowers grew there once and the grass was finer, but heavy grazing and burning has altered that, the globe flowers are gone and even the bog myrtle is bitten to its roots. Otters used to leave the river and the lake here and cross the road to holts in the hollow stones below Shepherd's Crag – they too are gone and only climbers remain. Farther down the lake at Kettlewell the meadow (now part privately owned scrub, part good public car park) used to be full of wild columbines in summer and even the next fields have changed. These are closely cropped by animals assisted, at times, by a big flock of Canada geese – the latter an introduction of doubtful blessing. There are more cormorants, too, on the lake nowadays and their droppings have killed at least one tree on an island – so it is not always people who make changes. Nor are all the changes negative: most of the eastern shore is open for people to enjoy and there are many paths through the fields and the woods by the lake although sadly the names are being forgotten – New Rivings, Black Steps, and Lord's Lands to name only a few. Nor do foxes get scarcer – this year's cubs are on the go and last week the local foxhounds went round and round within Great Wood, mazed by an abundance of scent for, as one follower says, 't'spot is wick wi' foxes'.

Keswick   7 December, 1970

Bee boles are small recesses in house or garden walls, and even sometimes in free-standing houses of their own, and were used to shelter straw bee-skeps against the weather before wooden hives were used. They are, of course, mostly very old and some are fallen into ruin. I saw three, very contrasting ones this week. The first set was at a beautifully kept farm near Carlisle but obviously of an earlier date than the farmhouse. There were six boles on a sandstone and brick wall, three smoothly arched above and three plain and square below on sandstone corbels – all facing south-west across a neat garden. No one remembered them in use. The second set could, I think, have been nowhere but in fell country in a sadly neglected little garth which was once a three-tiered, well-kept garden. They are in a dry, local-stone wall facing south; two are together, square and uncompromising, roofed with huge rounded stones, and the third is alone in a wall-corner. No one remembered them being used, either, except by pet lambs in spring for sleeping or sheltering places. The third lot were also unmistakably north-country, again in a dry-stone wall facing south-west, but this time as a recess from ground to wall top, ivied where its Borrowdale slate roof has fallen and oddly, this, the most broken, is the only one with a story of use. The farmer's wife remembered her grandfather's death and her grandmother sending her to lift the bees for her husband's passing – a variant, no doubt, of 'telling the bees' all that went on.

Keswick   1 February, 1971

There is a small flock of golden pheasants living very much at home in the undergrowth of a wood near here and, far separated, a solitary cock in another wood. They all seem peaceable enough and oddly suited to these woods so there was a question of putting a 'golden' hen in with the lonely one, but I am told that it would not do – murder could follow. Which very much reminds me of game-birds and their ways – one breeder who had too many cocks (they have to be kept well apart if loose at all) took one of his to put with some 'laal white hens' in an aluminium ark. He slipped it in, quietly, but almost at once the hens' heads were hitting the top of the ark like bullets and when the cock was finally enticed out with food he emerged with a beakful of feathers. The hens were never quite the same again. Nor are game-hens much better – one cuckoo-breasted hen drove an old lady a quarter of a mile down a fell path and though she dropped her bag on the way she was far too scared to go back. The same hen beat one of the local foxhounds into a wall-corner and rode a terrified sheep down the fell, clinging – full of fight – to its back. After all, game-birds are fighting birds, the descendants of ones said to have come to England, first, in the reign of Charles II and to have fought before him at Newmarket. Some of their traditional names ring like a chime of bells and are taken from common and unchanging things – Raven, throstle and cuckoo-breasted, Silver Duck wings, Red Duns, Hennies, Muffs and Tassels – all part of a cruder England where the cockers' toast was 'The Three Cs' – Cornwall, Cheshire and Cumberland.

Keswick   23 November, 1971

It is almost a year since Dr Max Hooper's article 'Hedges and History' was published in the *New Scientist*. It made many people take a closer look at hedges generally, things which until then had perhaps seemed just part of the landscape – homes for birds or sources of wild food. He puts forward the proposition that boundary hedges (and others) will have one species of shrub in every thirty yards for each hundred years of growth and he even tells of a hedge planted in AD 547 round Bamburgh in Northumberland. Here in the north-west, a land of fell and moor, there are almost as many stone walls as hedges, but there are old hedges too. Enclosure (a reason for some of the later hedges) was not perhaps as common here as on more valuable land, but in 1569 the Bishop of Carlisle enclosed Westward (probably by hedging) and in 1695 Celia Fiennes, travelling in the Lakes, wrote of 'enclosed land – hedgerows about looked fine'. There are still plenty of splendid hedges at the back of Skiddaw left over from the old forest roads of Inglewood, all havens for wild life, and a hedge to the west of Skiddaw which runs up from near Bassenthwaite past the Roman fort at Caermote could be, on this reckoning, five hundred years old on some of its length. Reflections on hedges came home last week when the boundary hedge of this garden had to be drastically cut to eight feet in height and slimmed to match. It is mostly thorn and holly, one thorn is almost a yard in diameter, and the line is shown on a map dated 1805 but it must, I think, be much older than that. But as Dr Hooper says, no hedge is just history. Birds, bumble-bees, mice, voles and weasels all use this one and its roots, and when it greens again next spring it should be ready for them.

Keswick   18 December, 1972

One of the books being given this Christmas is about beach-combing and how to identify what you find – but what about 'country-combing'? I have done this for much of my life and though, understandably, time has taken many of my treasures, some remain. They are mostly local, simple, and of little value to anyone except me but they serve as reminders of a time, a place or even, maybe, a person. Their time-span covers hundreds of years. I have, for instance, a large flake of volcanic rock discarded on the south scree in Great Langdale when Neolithic men were roughing out stone axes in that place. I have, too, a grainy piece of pottery from the Roman fort on Hardknott Pass and an undated stone, smooth and palm-fitting, which now serves (on a string) as a door weight. There is a handful of grey and stone-like hazel nuts dredged up by a spring storm from the sunken forest off the south Cumberland coast on a wild day in spring, when the sound of the sea and crying of the nesting gulls wove into the wind's cry. A mixture of discarded birds' feathers – nightjars, short-eared owls, falcons and a varied lot of ducks and small-birds' feathers – comes from fells, lakes, and sea-marshes. A shed roe-deer tine reminds me of a summer's day in a green yew thicket on the Westmorland limestone but one of the (to me) most treasured things is an

ancient jawbone of a badger from a pile of earth outside a
local sett – a place where, over a stretch of ten years, I learned
almost all I know of the ways of badgers and their cubs.

Keswick   *26 February, 1973*

Last week's snow is almost gone, except from the fells, and
the birds sing early and late but the grass is poor, as yet, so
some of the fell-sheep go foraging in and out of the woods,
along the wall sides and into any fellside garden with an open
gate. These wanderers are mostly Herdwick or cross-bred
sheep and 'ratching' is part of their nature. Snow and bad
weather, as such, do not worry them for they are built to
withstand it all, being sturdy little beasts with a long outer
fleece, called 'kemp', and softer, finer wool nearer the skin.
Herdwick fleece is coarse and hard-textured as well as being
of light yield, and it was known to be so even as early as the
fifteenth century when it fetched only about five marks a sack
as against, say, twelve for Shropshire wool. This, however,
didnot stop the northern merchants trying to smuggle it out
to sell in Flanders by way of Foudrey in Furness – in defiance
of the regulations of the Staple. The fleece may be coarse but
it is hard-wearing and thetweed from it, in its natural
spectrum of browns, is well-nigh indestructible. Indeed, a
local tailor, on making a skirt of it, told his client to name it
in her will, it would outlast her. At this time of the year it is
food (or lack of it) that sets the sheep to ratching and they
have not changed, it seems. Clarke, writing his *Survey of the
Lakes* in 1787, says Herdwicks 'live where the mountains are
very high as in Borrowdale, Newlands and Skiddaw – where
they have no hay for them in winter – and they lie out on the
very tops of the mountains in winter as well as in summer' –
unless, as now, they see a good garden in prospect.

Keswick   *19 November, 1973*

E. T. Connold's remark in his work on British oak-galls that
'the British oak is the abode of a vast concourse of
dependants', can seldom be more demonstrably true than it
now is. This is an abundant year for acorns and oak-galls in
the lower woods, birds feed in the canopy and small animals

on the woodland floor – only humans are lacking from the concourse. There is, however, a different aspect in the precipitous, relict oak woods 1,000 to 1,500 feet above the Newlands Valley. There was little sign of life there today and small wonder for there was snow on the tops and icy gusts of wind tore down the fell – strong enough to overset anyone caught off-balance outside the wood. The oaks, too, give only sparse shelter for they are old, at best only fifteen feet tall, and now many of their leaves are fallen. There are, however, some acorns this year which is unusual but – in contrast to the lower woods – there are almost no galls. Indeed the only 'spangles' on the fallen leaves are glittering drops of melted sleet. There were no birds about, only some disdainful, mountainy sheep who, in the past, have been blamed for the lack of regeneration. Now some of the Keskdale wood is fenced against them and it will be interesting to see the effect for there is a well-authenticated theory that oak does not regenerate under mature canopy – Keskdale is indeed mature, if thin. It is interesting, too, that there are small oaks outside the wood where the heather is deep; they have probably sprung from acorns left by jays and rooks energetic enough to fly so high for so small a reward.

Keswick   *18 November, 1974*

Farmers are sometimes taken as pessimists, complainers, a label most Cumbrians (including me) would reject – especially in the Lake District. After all, sheep-farming on the high fells is the staple here and mountain weather and sheep make a man a philosopher – or nothing. However, this year gives real cause for complaint. Seldom have the fells been more sodden, grass so poor and prices and prospects are grim, too. Sheep at Troutbeck sales which, last year, fetched about the twelve-pound mark are, this year, barely above three pounds, and a long and chancy winter lies ahead. But all is not gloom, cheerfulness breaks in, even on a dull November day like this with mist and cloud low on Helvellyn and the moor – seen from the farm kitchen window – made sombre brown and purple with rain and dusk. The wood fire crackles and flames in the grate, there is a warm smell of ironing in the air and the soft thump of the iron (even if twelve sheets await a better washing day) makes a descant to the voices. Apples, unlike grass and hay, are plentiful this year and must be stored outdoors in a hog (a clamp) lined with straw. Recipes for sweet pies made with mutton, fruit, and brandy – robust forerunners to the present-day mince pies – are discussed but, as so often, the talk turns to families and friends. These are not always one and the same. Some are remembered with wry amusement like the farm wife who is a 'chitterwallit' (an aimless talker) or another who goes gaustering on (laughing needlessly) or with affection like kindly Mary who always means well but who, however, does not always 'flee when she flaps her wings'.

Keswick   30 December, 1974

Scent, in summer, is something taken for granted; it is almost always there by day or by night – at least in the country. There is, then, a consciousness of a breathing, living world around you – but what about winter? Now that the shortest day is passed and the year is on the turn in a shifting pattern of storm and calm the chill midwinter has already a slow beat of returning life. Go out into a cold winter's morning, especially before first light, and almost at once, even within sight of other dwellings you are on the verge of that second world where man is only a minor thing. I wandered out this morning, picking up the day's milk as I went from the stone step where the milkman had left it – he is an early riser, too – while it was quite black, quite still, with the air milder and the wind fallen at last. An invisible spray of yellow flowering jessamine combed my face and all about me the earth breathed out the cold scent of winter, of sodden ground, dormant plants and the first wild sweetness of witch hazel and winter honeysuckle. The stars were clear for the first time for many nights and, though there was a faint hint of light to the east, the robin who, nightly, roosts above the step slept on, undisturbed. Brown owls hunted and called down the valley. But not all of winter's scents are of witch hazel or sleeping earth – there is fresh muck on the fields and one farmer's wife I know especially relishes the strange, rotten-sweet smell of a turnip field in a frost. But, since the crop is a good one, who can blame her?

Keswick

17 November, 1975

November in the country is an exhilarating time of the year, a time to look forward to, when the emptiness of the landscape, as the bare tree shapes stand forth and the rocks emerge as the bracken falls on the fells, is enhanced by the extreme clarity of the light. The soft blue shadows of summer are gone, shadows and sunlight are cooler now and have more depth but the sun fell strongly one day lately on the overgrown hedges which line the rising lane to the Castle Rigg stone circle. It picked out almost one at a time, it seemed, each red rose-hip, each turning bramble leaf, shadowing the still-vivid green in the hedge bottom and the few late golden buttercup flowers. Both the pale-grassed ridge of Helvellyn and the cone of Mell Fell to the east were sunlit too, but between them hung a truncated shaft of rainbow, bright against a thunderous dark sky. November for farmers, however, is not all rainbows and rose-hips. It is a very busy time of the year, if less evidently so than hay-time or harvest. There is always a lot of ditching to do, the cows are to be got in for winter and the sheep to be gathered down from the fell before the tups are loosed with them towards the end of the month. The hoggs, this year's lambs, used traditionally to be sent to the west coast – Solway or Morecambe Bay – to winter, but now a lot of them have to stay at home. The owners of the coastal land find it pays better to buy their own lambs to feed and to sell before April – the month when the fell hoggs would be going home. Times change, indeed.

Keswick

29 December, 1975

Cumbrian people talk about 'the dark days before Christmas' and these days often last well into the New Year but they do give time to look about the quiet countryside. The lengthsman sweeping up the last of autumn's wet leaves can lean on his brush and turn over the local news – old so-and-so is 'nobbut poorly', a frosty night is ahead and the price of next year's seeds is shocking. The man who wanders over the high farmland has time, too, to prop his gun on the wall and deplore the scarcity of wood pigeons (no acorns) and the almost total lack of hares (no doubt partly due to him) and the fact that moles are very active here, now. He says he had a pair of real moleskin trousers when he was a lad but, 'T'bloody things stank when wet.'

The emptiness of the winter landscape is quite illusory, even apart from the rare human and the ubiquitous sheep. I walked up the beck which runs out of Thirlmere today and found the sound of the wind in the bare trees and the rush of the water company enough. A pair of mallard planed down the stream to alight almost silently on a long pool and a dipper bobbed, this way and that, on one of its favourite stones. Dippers sing by day or night in winter or spring even in the most dismal weather and this one fled up the curve of the beck, singing, to fly directly under the water's surface and rise, seconds later, with something in its beak. The badgers, too, under the fell are active – unusually so for December – perhaps they also feel that winter is no time to be idle.

Solway Firth   *23 February, 1976*

The gales in early February scoured the saltings on the Cumbrian coast, ripping some of the sea-washed turf from its peaty bed, leaving all manner of wrack and many small, light-reflecting pools in the greening grass. These pools, this evening, gave back a silver shine and the Solway Firth was silver too – only blue where the declining sun lay along the Scottish side. The tide was far out and the birds with it and, inshore, a few shelduck, oystercatchers, a black-tailed godwit, and some curlews, whose voices rippled along the mud flats, was all there was to see. The thick gorse bushes, only lightly sprinkled with yellow bloom, and the wintry grass looked dark by contrast, but they made a perfect background for a quartering short-eared owl. Who said that an owl is just a flying cat? I cannot remember, but this owl, like any good cat, was a superb hunting machine – silent and deadly, it dipped and checked in flight watching every inch of the ground. Eventually it settled on a fence post, turning its head almost full circle so that the feathery rim of its face and the line of its body were outlined in silver against the light. There must be a good crop of voles and mice along the shore now for three short-ears were working along quite a short stretch and, as we watched, a fox went past on the landward side. It, too, was hunting, and, like the owls, it looked very much at home.

179

Keswick

The rough track up the fell to the ruined cottage in its ring of
green bogs and heathery wastes, a thousand feet above the
sea, is at present more of a stream than a track in places, but it
was once the vital link between cottage and valley and it is
still a place where the past seems very near. The buildings
were abandoned over fifty years ago and now there are only
ruins – perches for kestrels and scant shelter for sheep – but
the turf about them keeps its quality, close-cropped and
green. Today a thin mist lay across the fell, but this is,
however, never a sombre place even on a November day, the
dark heather and the pale nardus grass seem to gather light to
themselves but it was unusually quiet – all the sheep were
gathered down to the farm at the fell foot yesterday for an
autumn overlook and for the tups to be loosed to the ewes.
The cottage was always occupied by shepherds and their lives
are well-nigh forgotten now. There was a young, newly wed
couple with so little to take-at that the man had to carry their
coal up the long climb a sack at a time on his back but, later,
there was a family of nine merry children who went past the
farm before eight o'clock in the day, summer or winter, and
dawdled home playing up the beck in summer dusk. The last
man doubled as beck watcher and shepherd and was the
worst poacher for miles – there are still brown trout in the
beck but the only poacher is a heron.

Keswick

A wild-goose chase often has rewards quite unrelated to its
original goal. This happened lately when a rare flower was
reported near Penrith, and even though the message sounded
improbable it seemed as well to go and look. Itwas a damp
afternoon with cloud low on the ridges of Blencathra, and
shot throughwith stray sunlight which turned the wet rocks
to silver and the dead bracken to fire. The plant (as expected)
was a comparatively common garden one but the rest of the
afternoon made the cause well worthwhile. There was a
remnant of warmth in the sun and more than a remnant of
colour left in the village gardens in spite of rain and gale, and
there was time, too, to lean up on a low wall on the way
home and admire the thicket of sprouts, the ranks of leeks

and their edgings of marigolds. My sprouts this year have suffered with cabbage fly, so the owner of the garden told me to stick lengths of rhubarb below each small sprout next year on planting. Her friend said his potatoes had been riddled with small black slugs – the sort you seldom see except in potatoes – so I offered my time-tried habit of crushed egg-shells, thickly strewn under the potato seed. There was a lot else to talk about, too. It seems that a woman down the village is plagued with arthritis and though she may not have a cure at least she has an alleviation – willow (salix) leaves. She gathers them before they get too tough, dries and crumbles them to eat, year-long, sandwiched between bread and butter. And what do they taste of? 'Nowt,' I was told, 'except if they speak back – then they taste of kippers.' Well, if they help arthritis and kippers stay the price they are, a lot of us will be heading for the willow groves and, after all, willows and aspirin have the same chemical in common – salicylic acid.

Keswick   *5 December, 1977*

The main railway line and the M6 motorway run almost parallel, about three miles south of Penrith. Islanded between them and seemingly forgotten is the village of Clifton. But is it forgotten? Perhaps not, because Clifton Moor was the site of what is sometimes called (too grandly) the site of the 'last pitched battle on Englishsoil'. The Jacobite army under Prince Charles Edward had abandoned their uprising and their march on London at Derby on 6 December, 1745, butit was not until 18 December that the Duke of Cumberland and his heavier troops caught up with them at Clifton. It was not much of a battle, more of a skirmish between tired and hungry men and, like many such, bordering on the ridiculous – bitter though it was. For one thing, several officers on both sides had been to school at Mr Wilkinson's school – (for young gentlemen?) at nearby Lowther. There is an inconspicuous headstone in the churchyard to the men of Bland's Regiment, ten in all and mostly dragoons, but where are the Scots? They rest under a great oak, the Rebel Tree, south of the village. No one now knows how many died, for their remains were only found when the railwaywas built over a century ago – men from the Glens, men from

Edinburgh, far from home. Today, in the December dusk, the oak let fall a shower of gold and yellow leaves, a strangely English covering for Scottish dead.

Keswick   13 November, 1978

The change into winter was slow this year, held back by gentle October weather, but the ferocious storms in mid-November changed all that and left most of the trees leafless – except the oaks. It is astonishing how they have hung on to their leaves; the old oaks on the little hill below here groaned and creaked in the gales but they are still brown and green and gold. Acorns lie thickly under some of them. Things are different in the high-level oak woods and this is my time of the year to go to the Keskadale oaks in a narrow, precipitous cleft near the head of the Newlands Valley where roughly fourteen acres of short, sturdy sessile oaks (none pedunculate like the lowland oaks) are spread along the fell between 1,000 and 1,400 feet. This is a well-known, well-documented wood, possibly coppiced long ago, possibly the remains of an ancient wood, but the question is: How will the oaks survive as time goes on? They, too, still have leaves, but much ragged and torn by the weather and, this year, they have no acorns. That was evident even from below for not a rook, nor a pigeon, was about and only the sheep – vacuum cleaners on four legs – ranged along the slope which, now, is a dangerous shifting mass of scree and mud from the beck to the wood and is only lightly anchored by thin gorse and turf. The farmer's wife had said that there was 'a laal nip in t' air', but up there it felt more like the claws of winter and I was glad to get down and follow the tree-hedge back to Rigg Beck. There is no lack of life and colour there – the pale green of next year's hazel catkins, grey ash stems and acid green crab-apples (thickly clustered) are mixed with an abundance of deep red haws with fieldfares quietly gorging against winter's coming.

Keswick   22 January, 1979

It is difficult, now, to predict the weather locally with any certainty but one of the first signs of change is the calling of the brown owls at night – the hardest nights of January frost (coinciding nearly exactly with the temperatures of 1963) were very silent and that, with thesnow and the moonlight, made even the familiar Borrowdale fells look menacing and strange. Each hour, each day, broughta differing beauty – the rising sun touched the summit of Scafell and, in turn, the summits down the valley with pink, with gold and finally with shining silver. Deep blue shadows lay in the gullies and the shadow-shape of Causey Pike was outlined across the breast of Grisedale. It has been a hard time for animals, there was a constant scribble of mouse feet in and out under the house (nightly parties?) and bird tracks everywhere. A pair of redpolls still linger to feed on the birch cones outside this window; the cones were late to ripen in the autumn – usually the birds are here by early September but this time it was late October when a big flock came. How do they know where to come, when the cones are ripe? I have recently come home from Derbyshire where the birches in the valleys and up on the moors are still with cones untouched – do they not get eaten, and why not? The moorland sheep there were scratching in the deep heather of the grouse moors for food; here the sheep – Herdwick or Herdwick-cross – stay even higher on the fells and 'scrat' in the nardus grass or the rush roots and thin heather (no grouse moors here) for a bite. Clarke's *Survey of the Lakes* saysthat the Herdwick sheep 'lie out on the very tops of the fells in winter as well as summer . . . if a calm snow falls the shepherds take a harrow and drag it over the heather or ling so that the sheep feed on its tops or the moss below.' The sheep on Walla Crag above here managed well, alone, in the snow but as their owner says, 'There's nowt wrang wi' t'weather – it'll change,' and so it has, but it is shuttle-cock weather.

Keswick   *19 February, 1979*

January was the sunniest month since September, and there have been many clear, sunny days in February, but very cold ones, so it will be a long time before the snowdrifts go from the higher land where they have been driven against walls and into gullies and hollows by the wind. The tops look Himalayan rather than Cumbrian. The moor and the rocks are clear of snow, dun-coloured in the sharp light, but the drifts point up all sorts of shapes and oddities, almost unnoticed in greener months. If you look, for instance, across the valley from the A66 to the wide expanse of land which girdles the end of the Helvellyn range – Wanthwaite End and Wolf Crag – you see a multiplicity of patterns, white on brown. Sheepfolds are circles of white; one big enclosure edged with green rushes in summer is easier to see now, and the old road over to Matterdale glitters icily in the sun. Tracks and sheep-trods lead up to them from the valley and one track goes diagonally up the face of Wanthwaite crags to a sheepfold over the ridge. But it is in moonlight that the mountains and high land come into their own. The moon was up tonight before the sunset was gone – silver in the east, gold in the west with ice-blue clarity above Scafell. The light died quickly from the ridge of the Castle Rigg stone circle and though a dense bank of cloud shut off the Pennines it never rose to the face of the moon which sailed serenely up with a star beside. The stones were starkly black against the grass and the blown snow – there may be theories as to what this place was, what its purpose – but now is its time with not a bird or a beast stirring, onlythe Valkyrie whistle of the east wind through the thorn and the wire fences – and all one's clothes.

Keswick   *10 December, 1979*

Daylight comes slowly now but it soon shows pools of water lying in the fields below here which have never quite gone from the earlier storms which roared up the valley, howled through the oaks and hit the house front with frenzy. Yet, astonishingly, some oaks keep their leaves although all loose growth seems to have been swept away, leaving the fields and fells empty even of people – so the real owners are bolder and more in evidence. A golden eagle has been in the next valley and though the red-deer bucks are over the rut, thin and gaunt, their work done for this year, the foxes' year is just beginning and they are bold indeed. There are, this year, simply too many foxes. The last hard winter often prevented hunting for the local fell foot-pack and by spring places were alive with young foxes. There is, it seems, a real love-hate feeling for foxes from some hunting farmers. The milkman who comes at mid-morning, leaving home before sun-up, refers to foxes as 'Matey'. 'There was Matey when I went to gather the cows, popping up on the wall in daylight to stare as bold as brass.' Another farmer said a few years ago, as we stood in the centre of his flock of sheep, who steamed gently in the cold air and smelled of wet fleeces, that there had been three foxes playing in the field outside his yard that morning – and there is one nearer here, too. I saw him from my high window as he trotted purposefully from wood to coppice with his coat shining russet, his bib white, his tail-tip black, clear to see. Rooks followed him but at a careful distance. Occasionally he glanced back and turned, maybe to snarl, but he was much in command. Sorry, I like foxes, or do I hate them?

Keswick   *21 January, 1980*

I have lately retrieved a number of old stereoscopic glass slides and their elegant French viewer. These slides were taken by my family mainly between 1890 and 1902 and most of them are of rock climbing in Britain, the Alps, and the Dolomites, especially around Arolla. The ones of snow and ice have an almost uncanny reality and though the gear of those early climbers was very different, the mountains have changed only in varying degrees. The local valley views are perhaps unremarkable but some of the high mountain ones have surprises – for instance, Napes Needle with a figure suitably on top has a thick, shrubby growth near its base. There is nothing like that now. My father, in old age, used to complain that a lot of interest had gone from the more popular routes with ledges and holds cleared of debris and the rocks near-polished by nailed boots. He should see, say, the ground above Ashness Bridge (a too popular beauty spot) now, for not only is the grass gone but the earth itself is going fast and the rocks are bare. It is, it seems, the actual skin of the land which suffers worst and while the National Trust does its best to nurture the land it holds, it must be a discouraging battle at times. Not only are there more people; there are more animals too. Yesterday a neighbouring farmer told me, as we talked over his yard gate, pushed and rattled by young cows, that there are four times as many animals on that farm as there were in his fore-elders' time. That afternoon I met another farmer on the hill road, a small ageing man in an elderly car carrying fodder for his beasts in the valley. The car boot was open and piled high with blocks of hay until it seemed astonishing that the front wheels of the car were still on the road at all, and as I got home in the gathering dusk a helicopter crossed High Lodore, its lights winking, to leave more blocks for the sheep on the fell-tops before the real winter sets in – as it will.

Keswick   3 March, 1980

There was an afternoon this February which I shall long remember when bright sunlight washed across the limestone outcrops east of Saddleback (the mountain itself was dark, still snow-streaked), turning the beech trunks to silver and the dead beech leaves to fire. A cold wind stirred the withered grasses and fieldfares fled, calling, from hedge to hedge. There was a feeling of life and movement in the air. I had gone there, however, to finish over twenty-eight years of hunting and recording bee boles (places once used to shelter straw bee-skeps) in Cumbria. There should be more to find but I have covered a lot of land in those years and learned a lot, and not only about bee boles. But I have only once found someone who had 'told' bees and she was an elderly woman who had been sent as a child to 'lift' her grandfather's hives when he died – and then they would know he had gone. Few people have remembered boles in use either, although one old woman (now dead) told me twenty years ago in Borrowdale that her husband kept his skeps on 'something like a stone frying pan' in his boles. There were, and are, many uses for such handy recesses. They made safe, warm, sleeping places for the young lambs in a small garth below a farm at Thirlmere. A single bole in the Lyth Valley near Kendal had a plum tree on its wall so, on wintry nights, the bole was stuffed with straw, set alight, and left to smoulder to protect the plum buds. The last one on that sunny afternoon was in an old dry-stone wall in a moorland cottage garden where, over forty years ago, visiting grandsons were sent to wash outside in a tin basin balanced in the nearest recess. You had to keep your head well below the wall top, I was told, when an east wind blew. The honey bees here were on the early honeysuckle on 17 February, and soon after they thronged the first little purple crocuses intent on pollen gathering.

Keswick   *8 December, 1980*

Bleak November weather can be too much even for a
Cumbrian. Sometimes the only thing to do is to retreat
indoors – to a warm kitchen-fire and a topic started weeks
ago: horseshoes and iron in general. I have yet to find a
Cumbrian who will nail up a shoe with the points down. The
luck would certainly drain away. Indeed, it seems that only
blacksmiths themselves are entitled to display shoes down-
pointed, as on the badge of the Worshipful Company of
Farriers. But behind all this I sense an older trust that iron –
'cold iron' – is sovereign against evil and magic. Both of us,
talking, were old enough to remember how busy smiths
once were 'sharping' horses at the onset of winter. Holes had
been left in the fitted shoes and into these went the 'sharps' –
headed nails which gave the horses a better purchase on
wintry ground. We had talked the daylight away, and the
owls began to call in the edge of the wood below the fell
where, years ago, an old axehead – a 'squirrel' – was found in
a leaf-filled ditch. These axes had a very narrow cutting face,
and preceded saws. With them, two or even three skilled
men could work round the same tree and the butt, when
felled, was cigar-shaped and easier for horses to drag away
than a flat-ended one. It left a saucer-like depression in the
stump, which filled with rainwater to rot it naturally and
ward off fungus. But why a 'squirrel'? Was it the narrow-
shaped face or the shape of the butt, looking like a cone
gnawed by a hard-working red squirrel?

Keswick   *5 January, 1981*

The year has turned – even if the worst weather lies ahead. At
least there is time in these slow-changing weeks to decide
what to do in the coming months. I intend to pursue more
distant field names while they are remembered. This
countryside is fortunate, it still has its stone walls and a lot of
hedges, so the shape of many old fields is constant. There are
people with long memories, too. Many pieces of land justify
their names on ancient maps by shape – Long Wall, Long
Croft, Wood Edge, and so on, but why should an odd-
shaped corner field be called Santa Claus? Names change;
fields I knew in childhood as the Orchid field, the Cowslip

field have no flowers now, only grass. The Pig field even then had no pigs but a wealth of dog-daisies and hay in July; it has houses now. Names change, sometimes, with a new owner. 'Virily' in 1805 became Jonathon field in the next generation. One wonders who named Ruskells, and what does it mean, or Tim Field and Mary Close? Many are self-explanatory like Mellbrigg where dark water flows and water mints grow. Toad Pots, nearby, is a birchy swamp where toads will come in spring. Some of the land at the head of Bassenthwaite Lake are well named – Moss, Pickle, and Beckstones. But Froth and Wet lands are at the water's very edge and, today, are well under it.

Keswick   *16 February, 1981*

There was, most unusually, no one at the farm this morning and somehow as soon as you walked into the wide, cobbled yard there was a feeling of emptiness. Even before you rounded the house end you knew that no one would answer a knock on the iron-studded door. A line of washing sailed between black, bare damson branches in the orchard and snowdrops nodded in the grass. Cats came to greet me who are usually asleep by the fire or mousing in the haymew at that time of day. It was all mine to wander in – yards and barns – already well known but always offering surprises in their stones, re-angled in differing light. The longest barn was a brewery once and its south-facing wall, seen from the outside, has a bewildering pattern of filled-in doors and windows, seemingly all done by different hands at different times. Indeed, some of the small doors are a third below ground level now since the ground was raised some years ago. The slope rises at its north end and here three tall stone steps take you up to a gallery across the width of the building and into half-light under rafters swagged with cobwebs and old birds' nests. All four lids of the old corn bin stood open, a scoop in one, and there is everywhere still a feeling of friendly use even though no animals winter now, in the echoing dark below.

Keswick   *2 March, 1981*

Cloud lay along the snowy ridges of Helvellyn this morning but it was breaking on the crags of Wanthwaite End, delicately outlining each descending contour, each ledge and drop, with wisps of rising white mist. Hoar-frost rimmed the fields in the river valley and there was a skim of ice on the pools in the hollows where, mercifully, no frogs have yet come. They often get caught by late frosts in these shallow, spring-bubbling places where the cresses are greening. The river ran quietly, barely murmuring in its gravelly bed. Here, too, there is green – the strong, convoluted leaves of water-dropwort still below the surface and the paler spikes of flag iris just breaking above it. A pair of mallard rose, quacking indignantly, and fled downwater. I had gone to see what was going on in the badger setts and was pleased to find that the fields are not occupied by the usual herd of pushy, over-playful cows but by fell-sheep – as quiet as anyone could wish. That augurs well for nights to come, as does the fact that there is a lot of digging at the setts. No fox, I think, would be as energetic as that, preferring to take over what someone else has dug when possible. But the foxes are legion this year. Indeed, the young farmer over the fell says that there were eight in his intake one evening lately and someone had seen ten there next morning. 'T'buggers 'ull be hunting us next,' he says. And to whom, then, should one wish success?

Keswick   18 January, 1982

No one can say what the next day will bring this January – icy blizzards, sudden thaws, or some perfect days of sun and frost. The frost deepened early this afternoon and the setting sun glittered on icicles pendant from gate bars, on hawthorn berries already encased in diamond, and on the stiff, silvered mosses on the walls. As the sun sank it left an alpine glow on Helvellyn's snowfields. Wanthwaite End, Saddleback, and Skiddaw kept their rose-light a little longer until deepening blue shadows crept up their slopes, and then mountains and valley were given over to winter's bite. The snow squeaked and crunched underfoot, and even small drifts had to be negotiated with care: the east wind plays tricks with snow. Fifty sheep were lately dug out of this stretch of fell after eleven days and, though most survived, some did not. The rest are down near the farm now with hay bales and water. There was warmth by the hearth in the farm; winter stayed outside. I was given a small glass of cherry brandy, homemade from morello cherries grown in the orchard over the road, and its colour was not cherry, not ruby, but rather the transmuted glow of summer. The farmer was coming carefully round the barn-end when I left, carrying two slopping buckets of water for his sheep. He put them down on the snow and paused to talk – his bare hands not seeming to feel the cold, and mine were kept warm by a small parcel of 'two mince pies for your tea'. It was getting dusk but the moon was risen over the fell, and a bright star shone in the south when I got home to my own fireside.

Keswick   *15 February, 1982*

There is as I write a pair of magpies on the birch outside the window. They came in the snowy weather to the shelter of the dark spruces and now they are seldom away, seldom apart. At present, one watched intently by the other is prising something out of a cache between the tree trunk and an ivy stem. Both, lately, have taken to hiding treasures in there and this one looks like a chop bone – doubtless well ripened. Magpies have, here, in the past robbed nests, killed nestlings and been generally villainous – but how to be rid of them? They, like foxes, must live, too, and can provoke a love-hate relationship. My liking for them began long ago with a young one, parentless, who hand-reared grew strong, independent and thievish. Its favourite game was to sail down silently from the wood to tweak any sleeping cat's tail and be off. It wisely went wild in spring. Two years ago a pair settled here but then I appealed for help. Eventually a man arrived smelling strongly of something like Stockholm tar. He came in, took his ancient cap off, sat on it – he saw the 'pies outside and grinning cheerfully damned all vermin and all naturalists (me?) who might protect them. He went down to the spruces alone and stood there, unmoving, for almost twenty minutes seemingly lost in contemplation. When he had gone, still grinning, there was no sign left and nothing to show that he had been – but the magpies did not come back. Was it his very presence, his smell, or are magpies really prescient? He may be needed again shortly.

Keswick   *22 November, 1982*

Pack-horse roads, green roads, corpse roads and miner's paths are all part of this fell country and often one track served all purposes, using the contours of the land and the saddles between the valleys. The track above Glenderterra Beck between Lonscale Fell and Blencathra is an old and valued friend of mine. I well remember, long ago, accompanying my grandfather and my father up the valley as they 'rang' small hammers delicately on the hornfelded Skiddaw slates, for this is where, earlier, my grandfather had collected the 'musical stones' for his rock band (a sort of stone xylophone) to amuse visitors to Keswick. Indeed, he had had a small, secret cache in the higher ghyll to bring down with a horse cart and the help of two young, strong and more or less willing sons – a whole day's toil. The now-disused lead mine by the beck was only recently abandoned, in my youth, but already some adits were flooded, no place for adventurous children. Then there were shepherds or keepers in the old house out on Skiddaw 'forest'. In the twenties my father used to go up the valley and down Dash Falls to the north with Hugh Walpole who was getting the lie of the land for one of his Herries books. The Fortress is not far away at High Ireby. Today there was no one but me, the diligently grazing sheep and a pair of ravens calling excitedly from the crag, drawn there by the strange near-sweet smell of carrion on the air. So I went alone, but never lonely in that place, to where the sunlit flood water overran the flat, stone bridge at Roughton Ghyll and on up again to rest in Sinen Ghyll – where the 'stones' began.

Keswick *2 December, 1985*

Cloud can do strange things in quiet December weather. A thick mist along the valley and the lake can deaden everything but, given a clear valley and a low cloud layer, it can travel far. A friend who lived her life on a farm near Thirlmere used to say that she could hear the bells of Crosthwaite church plainly – six miles away and in the next valley – if the conditions were right. It seems as if the sound rose, hit the cloud layer and echoed away southwards. The ring is an old one. The church-wardens' accounts in 1669 mention four shillings and sixpence a year for ringers and five shillings for a bell rope. In 1706 it was sixteen shillings with ale for Thanksgiving days and November the Fifth. By 1714 the Great Bell needed attention so it was taken down, sent by cart to Whitehaven and by ship to Dublin to be re-cast. Those accounts have almost forty items varying from 'one shilling the night the bell was cast' to one pound and sixteen for 'our diet, lodging, and washing our linen'. The grand total, belfry to belfry, was just over thirty-seven pounds and the bells rang for the King's Coronation in 1715. Six bells were rung in 1775 and change-ringing began. A Yorkshire man arrived in Keswick with a travelling circus although he was a shoemaker by trade. He stayed to follow it and to teach the art of change-ringing in the belfry. Ringers had discipline. A board still hangs in the church adjuring a man to 'have an upright heart' and there are many fines for wrong-doing – eightpence for ringing with spur or hat or for an overturned bell. Times and bells may have changed but many of the names of those old ringers can still be met in the flesh in a Keswick street today.

Keswick   *24 February, 1986*

My 'new' cat is getting his bearings well. I said in November that I would not have another cat, parting with the last was too hurtful. That resolution is weakened after Christmas, however, to . . . maybe, in spring with winter gone. But winter had certainly not gone one cold January dusk when a fourteen-month-old kitten-cat arrived, unexpectedly, in a vet's carrier. He had lost his home and he was striped like his predecessor – in fact I was hooked. He is finely marked, dark with rabbit grey and with a tawny glint, too, especially on his shantung-silk underpants. He is as wild as fire. Today, in the dark spruces below the garden he saw birds foraging in the undercover and, instantly, he was flattened to the ground and his backend beginning that waggle which precedes a rush. He was not, however, the only hunter – silently, a brown owl swept low over both our heads so neither cat nor owl got anything. It was most frustrating to a young cat and in high dudgeon he shot up the nearest spruce out of sight but not hearing. A pair of magpies were there too and their outraged shrieks rent the air – a cat in their tree was just too much. Jackdaws joined in but the cat was totally at his ease and, unmoved, repaying an old score for his predecessor who was unnerved and harried in his youth by those same birds or their forerunners. This cat came down leisurely, his crampons (especially the back ones) working well; only in the last few feet did he drop into a spiny bramble thicket. The evening had to be spent getting the spruce resin out of his paws and his ruff. I look forward to spring.